ART AND ITS SHADOW

ART AND ITS SHADOW

MARIO PERNIOLA

Translated by
Massimo Verdicchio

Foreword by Hugh J. Silverman

continuum
NEW YORK • LONDON

CONTINUUM
The Tower Building, 11 York Road, London SE1 7NX
15 East 26th Street, New York, NY 10010

www.continuumbooks.com

This English translation first published in 2004
English translation © Continuum 2004
Foreword © Hugh J. Silverman 2004

First published in Italian as *L'arte e la sua ombra*
© 2000 Giulio Einaudi s.p.a. Torino

British Library Cataloguing-in-Publication Data
A catalogue record for this book is available from the British Library.

ISBN 0-8264-6242-1 (HB)   0-8264-6243-X (PB)

Typeset by Aarontype Limited, Easton, Bristol
Printed and bound in Great Britain by The Cromwell Press, Trowbridge, Wiltshire

Contents

Foreword:
Perniola's Postmodern Shadows

Hugh J. Silverman

In 1936, two of the most important statements in twentieth century aesthetics – Martin Heidegger's *Origin of the Work of Art* and Walter Benjamin's *The Work of Art in the Age of Mechanical Reproducibility* – were produced. Five years later, Mario Perniola was born in Asti (northern Italy) during the Second World War. What is remarkable about the *Origin of the Work of Art* is that Heidegger was attempting to ask not about the essence, but the origin of the work of art. And each time he attempted to define a determinate origin – the artist, or the work, or even art itself, he would find that the origin was already somewhere else. At best, the origin delineated a circle – a hermeneutic circle – which would constitute the place of truth – the disclosure or coming out of concealedness that happens in the event of the artist's relation to the work and to art. Art would at best be circumscribed by a frame, a *Ge-stell*, a stand-in or stand-out, that would delimit what was included in the realm of the work of art and what was not.

Curiously, Benjamin's account of the work of art in the age of mechanical reproducibility also tries to delimit the role of the work of art, but in this case instead of seeking a disclosure or truth to the work, he is concerned with what happens when the work of art is reproduced, photocopied, multiplied, readily available in a wide variety of contexts without any one piece having exemplary or originary status. This meant that the splendid *aura* that was so important to the traditional work of art was radically undermined. With the film or other forms of mechanically reproduced works of art, no particular instance had primacy, no version had any more value than any other. Each number in a lithographic series would have the same significance as any of the others. Each copy of a film would cost the same as every other copy. No instance would have any more of an *aura* than any of the others. Loss of the *aura* was a loss of uniqueness, loss of originality, loss of elitism.

Neither Heidegger nor Benjamin took the framework (*Ge-stell*) or the *aura* as the theme of their inquiry. In each case, the framework or the *aura* were aids in understanding the work of art in its essence or in its multiplication. For Perniola however the framework or *aura* is precisely what is thematized. The *aura* is the theme, topic, question to be explored in Perniola's *Art and its Shadow* (Einaudi, 2000). Perniola calls it a 'shadow'.

I

Shadows have a long history in philosophy. Plato thought that for those humans living in his allegorical cave, who have not seen the solar illuminations of the good, the beautiful, and the true, shadows were the only actuality available to them. Only the philosopher-kings would have direct access to the knowledge of the ideas of the good and the like. Dante in his *Comedy* imagined shadows or shades as populating his vision of Hell. Shades were the remnants or traces of the bodily existences and the sins for which they were being punished in Hell. But in each of these cases, shadows were taken to be a kind of reality, an existing world that humans must confront.

In more recent times, philosophers and their shadows were particularly significant. Maurice Merleau-Ponty (in 'The Philosopher and his Shadow' from *Signs*) thought of Edmund Husserl as casting a phenomenological shadow over all important philosophical research that followed in his wake. Merleau-Ponty himself thought of Husserl as the guide – his Virgil – who could provide the best possible account of how the world appears perceptually. Even here, the shadow was – as with Heidegger's *Ge-stell* and Benjamin's *aura* – the constitution of a reality, a marginal but significant limit to experience. In Heidegger's case, the *Ge-stell* was crucial to the experience of the work of art. In Benjamin, the *aura* gave the work its individuality and its authenticity – features that he thought were elitist and could not reach the masses as could mechanically reproducible works of art.

Nearer the end of the twentieth century, Jean Baudrillard took the shadows – for example in the first Gulf War – as the simulations that mark our everyday reality. For Baudrillard, we live among the simulacra and take them to be the only reality there is or can be. With Baudrillard, the shadows had become – as they painfully are again (and I write now in the phase of the coalition invasion of

Iraq) – the figure in place of the ground. Images and narratives had become only shadows, delineations of a fiction taken for reality. The outside had become the inside, appearance had become reality, TV images had become the narrative of what is – there is nothing outside the images – even the death and dying of war had become – as it did in the Vietnam War – images on a screen (and those who actually died achieved their end and glory by a report on the TV screen). 11 September 2001 reinfused the images – the reality of simulacra repeated again and again on the screens. We lived with the shadows of the attack – and now another set of attacks – more shadows – more attacks.

II

For Perniola, the shadows are neither the images on the cave wall, nor the hellish shades of Dante's inferno, neither the afterglow of the great philosophers, nor the *aura* that constitutes a work of art as a commodity of great value. For Perniola, the shadows are more like the Heideggerian *Ge-stell* (understood in a postmodern way) – a framework or structure which is neither outside the work of art nor its disclosed truth. The shadows of art are not anywhere – neither the work nor its context, neither what is outside the work nor what is inside it. The shadows (in Massimo Verdicchio's superb translation) are 'not *above*, in the Empyrean of aesthetic "values" even less *below*, in the dark depths of the popular and the ethnic, that one can find a remedy to the banalization of art, but *to the side*, in the shadow that accompanies the works of art and the artistic-communicative operations' (Introduction).

The shadows for Perniola accompany, are located alongside, constitute a supplement to the work of art. They are not something else however. They do not have an independent existence of their own. They do not improve works of art, they do not denigrate them. They do not underscore works of art, they do not enhance their value. These shadows do not account for the 'disgust', 'banality', and 'ingenuities' that Perniola describes as accompanying the democratization of art (in Benjamin's sense). As such, in Perniola, the shadows acquire names such as *resto* ('remainder'), 'crypt', 'experience of difference', but above all 'the sex appeal of the inorganic'. Shadows 'stand' alongside works of art. They delineate the shape of works of art. And in the shadows come the 'more subtle and refined experience, more intense and attentive to the work' and to 'artistic-communicative operations.' But as Perniola points out, this is not something 'negative', for 'without artistic institutions and without mass-media communication, the shadow would vanish' (Introduction).

In effect, Perniola is providing an alternative reading of Benjamin's notion of the work of art in the age of mechanical reproduction, for instead of arguing for the democratization of art which has as one of its necessary consequences the destruction of the *aura*, he argues instead for a third regime of art. Instead of remaining content with the binary opposition between the *aura* with 'the cultural value attributed to the unique and lasting object, which favours an aesthetic experience based on a relation of distance with respect to the user, and the system fully secularized and disenchanted opened up by the mechanical reproduction of the work of art, which confers a merely expository value and initiates a relation of proximity with the public' (Chapter 5), Perniola offers the shadow of art as the place of this third regime. This third regime of art and aesthetic experience is 'characterized by reification, fetishism, and most generally, by the phenomenon that he himself [i.e. Benjamin] defined as "the sex appeal of the inorganic".' The sex appeal of the inorganic has become Perniola's recent trademark. Published contemporaneously along with *Art and its Shadow* is Perniola's *The Sex Appeal of the Inorganic* (Einaudi, 1994), also translated by Massimo Verdicchio (Continuum, 2004).

III

But what is the 'sex appeal of the inorganic' and what does it have to do with the shadows that we have been discussing? In Chapter 2, aptly entitled 'Feeling the Difference', Mario Perniola distinguishes three versions of this 'sex appeal' of the inorganic. The first version is one that he had already taken up in the volume that is published in English as *Engimas: The Egyptian Moment in Art and Society* (Costa and Nolan, 1990; translated by Christopher Woodall for Verso in 1995). The Egyptian version of the sex appeal of the inorganic is a 'neuter sexuality' nourished by the excitement of the natural mineral world. Here the environment is sensitized and the human is reified (with its 'fetishistic, sado-masochistic and necrophiliac interest in mummies and bondage').

The second version is characterized by *cyberpunk*. Here, electronic and cybernetic technology produces 'cyborgs' – those science fiction characters whose organs are replaced by artificial devices. This is the post-human and post-organic phase, where computers become the model according to which substitute sexuality is realized – as in cybersex. But its main interest is to develop 'neuter sexuality which is anchored in the philosophical experience of the *epochē*. As a suspension of judgement – a bracketing of what can be known (as Husserl put it, deriving his account from Sextus Empiricus, the Greek sceptic) – the *epochē* involves a disengagement from direct experience, from feeling of any real objects.

But the third version is indeed that which Perniola proposes when he argues for 'feeling the differences.' The shadows are felt differences. This is not abjection (as in Kristeva) nor is it a poetics of gore and trash. To the extent that the differences live, that is what Perniola elsewhere called 'transit' (see in particular his account of 'transit' in *Ritual Thinking: Sexuality, Death, World*, translated by Massimo Verdicchio and introduced by Hugh J. Silverman for Humanity Books, 2001). Transits are non-places that are incessantly between and in motion, that accompany objects, works, things, but which are felt as difference, as differend (in Lyotard's sense), as the zero degree of theory (in Roland Barthes's sense), as *Verneinung* or denial (in Lacan's sense), as the 'shock' of the real in the 'ambivalent and ambiguous experience of disgust' (in Perniola's sense) (see Chapter 1).

The shadows are the feeling of differences. And in Chapter 6, Perniola links this feeling of the differences with the remainder and the crypt. A remainder, as we know from Derrida's accounts, is a supplement, a left-over, a super-addition of sense, but not an alternative, not an opposite, not the other side of a binary pair. A remainder is like a shadow, it follows around what it adds onto. A remainder is a something more, a frame, an edge, but also a trace of what it remains from. Perniola stresses the standing, stability, steadiness, and resistance that is part of *resto* (a remainder). But there is also the fluid aspect. A remainder follows what it remains from and of wherever it goes. To aid his account, he draws upon Guy Debord and the International Situationists on the one hand, and on Joseph Kosuth's conceptual art on the other. Both produce a residue – the one where art ends up in philosophy and the other where philosophy ends up in art.

For Perniola, the sex appeal of the inorganic ends up in the crypt. A crypt is an enclosed incorporated or embodied space. It is separated from the outside, but in marking itself off from the outside, it is a 'hidden treasure that shines only in the dark.' The crypt is linked to Perniola's earlier account of the 'enigma' as transit. The crypt keeps the secret, blocks the outside from entering in, and establishes its own space even though it remains a relational, differential space, one that cannot be unravelled, dispelled, or dissolved without itself losing its status as a crypt, as cryptic. Hence, as Mario Perniola concludes this wonderful compendium of contemporary aesthetic and cultural theory, the crypt is a 'cemetery guard' that is 'made of guile, ingenuity, and diplomacy' (Chapter 6).

The crucial term in the title of this essay *Art and its Shadow* is the 'and'. The 'and' is what links and separates 'art' from its 'shadows.' The 'and' is the remainder, the crypt, the transit, the enigma, the sex appeal of the inorganic. The 'and' is neither part of the organic whole that is art nor anything like the illusory character of its shadows. The 'and' remains inorganic and yet it has an incredible sex appeal . . .

IV

The appearance in English of this critical essay in contemporary aesthetic theory only three years after its initial appearance in Italian marks an important departure and yet it augments and provides a valuable enhancement to *The Sex Appeal of the Inorganic* which had appeared six years earlier (in 1994). Both of these books are important developments from Perniola's work of the 1980s, in particular, *La Società dei Simulacri* (Bologna, 1983) and *Transiti* (Bologna, 1989). The main body of these two works are now available in the aforementioned *Ritual Thinking: Sexuality, Death, World.*

But just a few years before 2000 when *Art and its Shadow* first appeared, Mario Perniola published a long and substantial account of twentieth century aesthetics. In his *Twentieth Century Aesthetics* (Il Mulino, 1997 but not yet translated into English) Perniola thematizes five different twentieth-century accounts of aesthetic theory. These include (1) aesthetics of life (Dilthey, Santayana, Bergson, Simmel, Unamuno, Ortega y Gasset, Marcuse, Foucault, Agamben); (2) aesthetics of form (Woefflin, Riegl, Worringer, Florenskij, Panofsky, Focillon, Kubler, Elias, McLuhan); (3) aesthetics and understanding (Croce, Husserl, Hartmann, Gadamer, Cassirer, Jung,

Bachelard, Adorno, Merleau-Ponty, Jauss, Vattimo, Goodman); (4) aesthetics and action (Tolstoy, Dewey, Bloch, Gramsci, Lukács, Mukarovsky, Sartre, Kuki, Baudrillard, Apel, Habermas, Rorty, Bloom); and (5) aesthetics and feeling (Freud, Heidegger, Wittgenstein, Benjamin, Bataille, Blanchot, Klossowski, Lacan, Derrida, Deleuze). This compendium of aesthetic theories is, in particular, a kind of prelude to *Art and its Shadow* – or to put it another way, *Art and its Shadow* is itself the shadow of *Twentieth Century Aesthetics*.

This shadow of twentieth-century aesthetics now at the turn of the new century gives important insight into Perniola's own reading of the contemporary status of aesthetics. His lesson is an important one – namely, that remainders, crypts, shadows are the non-space that accompany art and give it meaning – not the content of the particular works of art that we confront in museums, in catalogues, in books, on the street, and in the electronic media. These shadows accompany each and every experience of art – as trauma, as disgust, as splendour, as grandeur, as exceptional ... as the sex appeal of the inorganic ...

Mario Perniola has carved an important space as one of the most significant theoreticians of aesthetic theory in Italy today. In giving an account of the shadow of the work as more important than the work itself, Perniola has offered a ground-breaking formulation. This is not to say that we must forget the major contributions of Gianni Vattimo and Umberto Eco – also students of Luigi Pareyson in Turin – but only that Mario Perniola, a younger member of Pareyson's cohort and a practising professor of aesthetics at the University of Rome (Tor Vergata), has been developing new ways to think about the postmodern spaces in which aesthetic theory has come to practise and disclose. *Art and its Shadow* as a supplement to his *Twentieth Century Aesthetics* on the one hand and as a complement to *The Sex Appeal of the Inorganic* on the other delineates just such umbral spaces. And we can surely anticipate much more to come ...

Introduction

The way in which we approach art today is often characterized by a great ingenuity that affects not only the majority of the public but also many professionals. This ingenuity is apparent in two different ways that at first sight seem opposite, that is, in considering works of art as essential to art or, on the contrary, in attributing to artistic operation the characteristics of immediate and direct communication.

The first aspect of this ingenuity identifies art with the work of art, which is seen as an entity endowed with a cultural, symbolic value or even just economical, autonomous and independent. It is the point of arrival of creative activity and constitutes the centre around which mediation is articulated, discourses are organized and fruition is focused. According to this point of view, what matters in art are the products on whose object-like quality no doubt is possible, such as paintings, sculpture, books, buildings, musical compositions, representations, film, videos. The object constitutes the essential, compared to which the productive process, the ideas of the artist, the mediation of the historian, the critic, the curator and the philosopher, even public reception, constitute something secondary and incidental. Art is supposed to possess a very definite identity, with respect to which everything else is secondary. After all, this is the perspective of the owner whether he is a collector, author, editor, producer, public or private.

But there is an opposite and complementary ingenuity which is also present today with special vigour. It consists in completely resolving art in life, placing it in a competitive relation with the instruments of mass communication, information and fashion. In this perspective, art loses every specificity, its message is not distinguishable from that of advertisement except for being self-promotional. What matters is the manifestation of a vitalistic relation that can be simply playful and gratuitous, or intended to acquire a value no longer on the art market, but on that of communication. Even in this case, mediation does not constitute an essential part of artistic transaction which points instead to its immediacy, which is entirely open and without secrets. It is as if the activity of the artist did not consist so much in producing a work, as action, or, better, a communication not subordinated to the attainment of a commercial or political end, or any other type, and emancipated from any other function other than that of reaching and eventually involving the public.

The two opposite lines meet in attributing to art a simplicity that in the former case is placed in the produced work, and in the latter, in the communicative operation. Naturally, the work appears to the supporters of artistic communication as a fetish, while the communicative operation appears to the supporters of the work of art as the manifestation of a tenuous vitalism. But in both cases the problematic of art is removed in favour of something much more banal.

The ingenuity of both positions is in the common presumption to capture art in its fullest light, as a well determined entity or as a communicative immediacy, ignoring the *shadow* that inevitably accompanies the work as well as the artistic operation. In other words, today more than ever, art leaves behind a shadow, a not so bright silhouette, in which is portrayed anything disquieting and enigmatic that belongs to it. The more violent is the light which one pretends to shed on the work and on artistic operation, the brighter is the shadow they project. The more diurnal and banal is the approach to artistic experience, the more what is essential withdraws and takes refuge in the shadow.

Art today suffers from a double simplification which is the result of the general process of demystification and secularization that involves all symbolic activities. On the one hand, it is levelled over the *works,* by leaving aside everything which is a condition of the existence of a work of art. On the other hand, it is levelled over *reality*, by leaving aside the thickness and the complexity of the real. In a many-sided era like our own, the world of art seems made up mostly of simpletons for whom art is resolved in its price and in the interpretation of its works, or in the effectiveness and the communicability of the message. All the rest, that is, what makes possible the category of art and the figure of the artist, is considered a useless metaphysical appendix which must be disregarded as an uncomfortable legacy from which one has to be freed as soon as possible, as a useless frill that oppresses the true life of art. In short, it is considered 'natural' that some objects are works of art and that some people are artists. Any other question seems superfluous.

This general levelling of art on the question of works of art and communication has provoked the reaction of those who claim for art the preservation of a special statute, rooted in the transmission of tradition and the solemnity of 'values'. However, they do not grasp the progressive aspect present in present-day gullibility and simple-mindedness, and they entrench themselves in the impossible defence of an artistic and aesthetic transcendence in which they themselves do not believe. As in other spheres of culture, in art, also, traditionalism is the braggart and, thus, does not constitute a remedy against gullibility and simple-mindedness but flourishes precisely on account of it and those it is able to deceive. In fact, reducing art to art works and to communication has even produced positive effects. It has not only made art more approachable for ever-greater masses of people and for the inexperienced individual incapable of grasping the difference between the real and symbolic dimensions, but, above all, it has widened enormously the boundaries of art by bringing attention to 'thingness' (*cosalità*) and to 'transit', which are notions ignored by conceptions of art that are too spiritual and too metaphysical. This is not to say that 'thingness' or 'transit' are simple or 'natural' experiences!

The error of traditional reaction consists in persisting to place what is worthy of interest, esteem and admiration *above* instead of *to the side*. It understands well the degeneration inherent in the democratization of art, namely, the transformation of great exhibitions in *amusement parks*, the character both violent and ephemeral of transgressive artistic operations, the predominance of quantity over quality, the poking fun at the public, the reduction of professionalism to managerial flexibility, the cynical utilization of artists and critics, the homologation of cultural products, the spread of a climate of unanimous consent around the *stars*, the disappearance of a critical ability, the lack of conditions for original growth and development, the disregard of excellence. But traditional reaction errs when it opposes to all these disadvantages an inflated idea of art based on aesthetic 'values' that no one knows how to characterize any more. It is not *above*, in the Empyrean of aesthetic 'values', and even less *below*, in the dark depths of popular and ethnic values, that one finds a remedy to the banalization of art, but *to the side,* in the shadow that accompanies the exhibitions of works of art and artistic-communicative operations.

The democratization of art, with all its ingenuities and banalities, with its blend of stupidity and fatuity, represents a point of no return in the history of culture. However disgusting and coarse its products may be, it is in its shadow that a much more subtle and refined experience, more intense and attentive to the work of art and to artistic operation, can be maintained and developed. The more art grows, the bigger its shadow becomes, the greater the spaces that it is not able to illuminate become. Therefore, this experience no longer recognizes itself in the metaphor of the underground but in that of the shadow. The shadow seems at first sight connected to a kind of esotericism, with some necessity for concealment and cautious and gradual manifestation. However, this relative esotericism does not originate from a strategy and not even from a propaedeutics, but from the nature of things themselves which requires a certain protection and safeguard, as well as prudence and discretion on the part of those who would like to enjoy them.

Therefore the shadow of art must not be thought of as something negative which is in a relation of antagonistic opposition to the *establishment* of art or with respect to the world of communication. Without artistic institutions and without mass-media communication, the shadow too would vanish. Nor can it be considered to be somewhat parasitic and servile. If anything, it is a reserve from which what is constantly in the limelight draws. Anyhow, to the nature of the shadow belongs the characteristic of disappearing as soon as it is exposed to full light. Here lies its *difference* with respect to institutional canonization and media transmission.

The ingenuity of the artistic *establishment* and communicative immediacy is largely revealed in the way in which they think about conflict. Generally, they tend to deny the existence of an opposition and set out the relations among different entities at play according to those models of reconciliation and harmony that have always belonged to ideological constructions. When this is not possible, the dialectics of positive and negative constitute the way in which the canon renews itself and vitalism achieves a new impulse. But the shadow does not fall in these types of trap. It remains extraneous and different. It is not the element of a more complex harmony, or the moment of a dialectic process that thrives on contradiction.

After all, ingenuity consists in pretending to defeat an adversary or reconciling with him, or taking his place. But the shadow does not place itself as an adversary, but, if anything, as the keeper of a knowledge and a feeling which it alone can reach, only to disappear when the full light wants to appropriate it. It implies a deeper experience of conflict than what the institutions and communication can achieve, and that is why it believes inevitable the establishment of *compromise formations,* without winners or losers. That is why it does not agree with the idealization of conflict and victory implicit in the dialectic. For the shadow, winning is impossible and to think of winning is naive.

These statements become even clearer when we refer to the contents of the chapters in this book. The first chapter discusses the return to realism in the experience of art today. It questions the category of the 'real' by distinguishing two aspects of this notion: the real as idiocy and the real as splendour. Now, the real as idiocy is suitable to designate many artistic manifestations of the *establishment* and mass communications, but these phenomena often bring with them a shadow that shines paradoxically and is endowed with a kind of magnificence. In any case, it is not possible to bring this splendour in full light, without dissolving it. It is only manifested in the shadow.

The second chapter takes its point of departure from two key ideas of traditional aesthetics, work and pleasure. Roland Barthes replaced them, respectively, with the notion of text and bliss. By further radicalizing Barthes's analysis we arrive at the notions of *neuter* and *epoché,* which can be regarded as the shadows of the work and pleasure. And, to be sure, the experience of the *sex appeal of the inorganic,* which is also the title of a fortunate book of mine, also belongs to the dimension of the shadow, where artistic doing and aesthetic feeling seem to coalesce.

The third chapter, in questioning the figure of Andy Warhol, whose activity represents the greatest success both in the sphere 'of the art of works of art' and in the sphere of artistic communication, shows how it is entangled in a quarrel that cannot be reduced in terms of a dialectic between positive and negative. Jean-François Lyotard was the first to formulate the paradoxical logic of *dissensus (différend).* The modern and postmodern are accompanied by a shadow in which the question of 'value' seeks refuge.

The fourth chapter, by exploring the borderline that goes from the film with images to the film without images, examines the possibility of philosophical cinema that goes beyond the boundaries of the didactic film without falling in the naive claim of providing an exact reproduction of reality. It is a matter of locating the viability of a new path, both philosophical and cinematographic, that can be posited in a territory beyond the distinction between reality and fiction, between documentary and narrative, and is capable of maintaining a relation with 'truth' without being levelled by the mere mimesis of facts. Naturally this 'truth' will be closer to the shadow than to a representation without veils.

The fifth chapter takes on the question of contemporary art with reference to sociological inquiry. Starting with Walter Benjamin's distinction between two systems of works of art, one endowed with *aura* and one characterized by technological disenchantment, we arrive at a third system which has a virtual character with respect to the paradigm being applied today. In fact, this third type has belied Benjamin's predictions and is constituted by a sufficiently incongruous mixture of aspects that come from the world of artistic inspiration, opinion, and the market. The third system of art, which is a kind of political economy of *grandeur*, can be thought of as the shadow that the contemporary paradigm brings along with it.

Finally, in the sixth chapter the focus is on two notions that have affinities with the shadow: *remainder* and *crypt*. If we keep in mind that the experiences of the Situationist's anti-art movement, conceptual art and the *Post human*, have considerably shortened the distance be-tween art and philosophy to the point that their destiny seems by now joined together, we would like to ask how is it possible to avoid the melancholy cynicism that characterizes both these cultural systems. One alternative can be found in the device of *cryptic incorporation*, which can constitute a defence with respect to the processes of normalization and standardization taking place in society, which appear either in the form of monumental institutionalization or of communicative vitalism.

Art and its Shadow

1

Idiocy and Splendour in Current Art

1. The 'shock' of the Real

In the artistic adventure of the West one can single out two opposite trends: one directed toward the celebration of appearance, the other oriented toward the experience of reality. The first trend has focused its attention on the notions of separation, distance, suspension, and has regarded the aesthetic attitude as a process of catharsis and de-realization. The second trend, on the other hand, has conferred special emphasis on the idea of participation, involvement, compromise, and thinks of art as perturbation, electrocution, *shock*. Roughly, I would place within the first trend, those who believe that the aim of art is to remove us from reality and free us from its weight; in the second one, I would place those who attribute to art the task of providing us with a stronger and a more intense perception of reality. These two opposite trends have confronted and fought each other throughout the cultural history of the West but neither has definitively succeeded over the other. Thanks to this dispute, however, they have always managed to renew themselves, introducing each time always new and original aspects and traits.

The first trend has found in the evolution of the means of mass communication a powerful ally. The idea of social spectacle, the poetics of the ephemeral, the expansion and commercialization of leisure time have encouraged the hedonistic and recreational aspect of time. During the 1980s, this was widely expressed in the recovery of the traditional forms of painting, literature, architecture and music as celebration of popular culture, as 'weak thought', 'post-modern,' 'trans-avant-garde.' Later, the notion of virtual opened up a new problematic that, at first sight, seemed to provide elements in favour of a de-realization and separation from the real.[1]

At the same time, however, we have witnessed the manifestation and the spread of an opposite artistic sensibility that has taken shape as a veritable irruption of the real in the rarefied and highly symbolic world of art. The attention of artists has focused on the most violent and most raw aspects of reality and, above all, the themes of death and sex have acquired greater importance. It is not a question, as in the past, of the most naturalistic representation possible of this reality, but of a direct exposure of events, poor in symbolic mediation, that provokes dismay, repulsion, if not outright disgust and horror. The categories of disgust and degradation force themselves arrogantly on aesthetic reflection which now finds itself obliged to abandon the ideal of a pure and disinterested contemplation in favour of a disturbing experience where repulsion and attraction, fear and desire, pain and pleasure, refusal and complicity are mixed and mingled. The body, thus, seems to acquire greater importance but the emphasis is no longer on the beauty of forms but, precisely, on what threatens and compromises its integrity both by means of penetration, dismemberment, dissection, and by means of prostheses, extensions, interfaces. In fact, the real that irrupts and upsets the world of art is not only the one rooted within the anthropological dimension but also, and above all, the one even more foreign and disquieting of technological and economic devices. The crucial moment of this extreme realism is, thus, the meeting place between human and machine, organic and inorganic, natural and artificial, impulse and electronics, people and commodities. The harsh reality that we are obliged to confront is the *cyborg*, the technological guinea pig, the living money, the human capital. The notion of virtual, which at first seemed connected to the spectacular and to the de-realizing tendency of art, acquires in this case the opposite meaning. The virtual body, invaded and disseminated in networks, becomes the object extremely other and disquieting, and irreducible to the imaginary and symbolic dimensions.

What characterizes this real is the coincidence of the greatest effectiveness and the greatest abstraction. In other words, it brings to its extreme consequences that process of alienation and estrangement that constitutes the motor of modernity. That is, we are not moving along on some marginal path, but, precisely, along the main road of Western thought in the most advanced point of its path, along a border that only asks to be crossed. Hence the eminently experimental and pioneering character of artistic experiences that today goes back to the category of 'realism'. To be sure, this realism that was defined as 'post-human' (Jeffrey Deitch), 'traumatic' (Hal Foster), 'psychotic' (by me), seems to have little to do with what up to this day was understood with this term. What has changed, however, is not the will to provide an exhibition of the real, but the very idea of the real, which today seems to us, at the same time and contradictorily, poorer and richer than ever. It can be read as extreme poverty and stupidity, that is, as idiocy, or, as extreme sumptuosity and surplus, that is, as splendour.

2. Idiocy of Today's Realism

The premise of today's realism is the wear and tear of all theoretical and critical coordinates on which contemporary art was founded. The aesthetic of the twentieth century, even in the great multiplicity and variety of its manifestations, can be considered on the whole as a development of the conceptual horizons opened up by Kant and Hegel. Now these horizons have been explored in all directions. After all, for some time now, the most innovative trends in philosophy considered aesthetics as a reductive and inadequate approach to the work of art. However, they have not succeeded in reestablishing on new bases the specificity of the aesthetic experience. An even greater deterioration has worn away art criticism. The problematic opened by the Vienna school at the beginning of the twentieth century has known an irremediable degeneration. In the best of cases, it generates a discourse that has only an occasional and fortuitous relation to the works of art and the artists. Most of the time, it does not go beyond commentary and advertising.

The collapse of all aesthetic and critical certainty leads to the opinion that it is possible to grasp the real without any theoretical and symbolic mediation. After all, the transformation of any object or image of everyday life in a work of art is a practice that has become self-evident starting with the neo-avant-gardes of the 1960s, but such a transformation required the celebration of the product through the intervention of the critic and its introduction in artistic institutions. The zero degree of theory, reached today, dissolves even this illusion because it removes any aura not only from the work and its author, but also from the critic and the institution. A Marxist saying goes: 'Without theory, there is no revolution', but it presupposes the saying on which modernity is founded: 'Without theory, there is no institution.' The zero degree of theory leads to a flattening of the existent from which none is saved. Today's extreme realism makes precisely this claim of showing the existent without any theoretical mediation.

But what is the real in its naked existence? The real deprived completely of any conceptual mediation? An existence completely deprived of essence? A reality devoid of any idea? A being absolutely independent of thinking?

The philosopher who asked himself these questions was Schelling, who defined the pure existent precisely as intransitive, immediate, unquestionable, immemorial, and groundless. As the Italian philosopher Luigi Pareyson, a great interpreter of Schelling, wrote: 'the pure existent is something opaque, which remains closed and recalcitrant to thinking, and refractory and impermeable to reason.'[2] It 'rises solitary and inaccessible as in an uninhabitable and inaccessible desert. It stands as a steep cliff impossible to attack, as a bare wall without holds, as a smooth and insurmountable wall'.[3] Similarly, the Slovenian philosopher Slavoj Zizek, another interpreter of Schelling, stresses the radical divergence, the ontological incompatibility between reason and the primordial real, which is radically contingent, and inaccessible to any theorization. Zizek demonstrates the radical affinity between Schelling's 'existent' and the notion of 'real' elaborated by Lacan.[4] And it is precisely Lacan who provides us with the possibility of formulating the poetics of extreme realism of the arts today.

As we know, Lacan differentiates between three fundamental psychic stages: the symbolic, the imaginary and the real. The last one is something radically different from the true. It is extraneous to language and to the symbolic dimension. In fact, it is precisely what resists symbolization. Impossible to symbolize and to imagine, it presents those characteristics of opaque irreducibility to thought that Schelling attributes to it. It is absolutely 'without cracks,' that is, it is alien to any dialectical articulation, extraneous to any opposition, including that between presence and absence.[5]

The encounter with the real generates anguish and trauma. In fact, the real defies all language and all categories. That is why for Hal Foster, trauma seems to be the most adequate notion to interpret today's art which is characterized, precisely, by a will to confront the viewer with something terrifying and despicable.[6] Actually, the disturbing object of art today, par excellence, is the corpse. It is the thing in which terror and degradation, repulsion and attraction come together and are confused in the ambivalent and ambiguous experience of disgust.

There is a strong temptation to view disgust as the main category of contemporary aesthetic. What is striking, above all, is the anti-thetical correspondence that is established with the notion of taste, the central category of eighteenth-century aesthetics. Today, the most acute observations on the notion of disgust are those of the Hungarian philosopher Aurel Kolnai. In his view, while anguish focuses on the subject, which finds itself in a state of danger and threat, and needs safeguard and protection, disgust is more clearly oriented toward the outside. Therefore, it has an 'intentional' char-acter (in the phenomenological sense) greater than anguish, thus making possible a greater knowledge of the object that provokes it. The disgusting asserts itself with a proximity and a contiguity which is lacking in both the distressing and in the hideous. It behaves toward us in a provoking manner, it approaches and moves against us, not only generating repulsion but also repressed attraction. What characterizes it is precisely contiguity, its capacity of penetration and contamination. Even for Kolnai the disgusting par excellence is the corpse, the greatest manifestation of putrefaction, decomposition, of passing from the living to the dead. It is for us something extremely near because it represents the only absolutely certain destination of our body. Reflecting on the characteristics of other disgusting objects, such as excrements, secretions, filth, worms, the insides of the human body, tumours and physical deformities, Kolnai arrives at the con-clusion that the essential of disgust consists in a life *surplus,* in an exaggerated and abnormal organic vitality that swells and spreads beyond any boundary and any form, and circulates by homogeniz-ing everything in a formless and putrid mass.

In itself life is not disgusting, only its obstinacy to remaining and spreading there where it should stop and cease. The disgusting is, precisely, the claim of the vital to swelling to the utmost and pollut-ing everything that comes into contact with it. This conception of the essence of the disgusting, as life immoderate and rebellious to any form, allows us to understand also the moral use of the word. In fact, what is disgusting is the interference of vital immediacy (such as drives and personal interests) in all questions that have an objective and formal character. The lie is disgusting because it is full of vital and emotional viscosity which is absurd and incongruous. Deceit is disgusting when it conceals under the mantle of ideals the cove-tous and muddled affections of the individual. Finally, cowardice is disgusting as it consists of the interference of an unhealthy and morbid vitality in situations that require the defence of a choice, the attainment of a goal, the fulfilment of a decision. According to Kolnai, economy pure and simple is not disgusting because it proceeds according to an abstract logic from which life is excluded a priori. It becomes disgusting when it hides behind the screen of values, of ideology, that is, of a deceitful and hypocritical affectivity. For instance, the institution of contemporary art becomes disgusting when it conceals its character as a market of luxury items behind the rhetorical exaltation of aesthetic ideals in which none believes.

There is no doubt that some aspects of art today can be interpreted according to the categories of trauma and disgust. Yet, Kolnai's analysis on the nature of disgust begs some questions. The real, of which Schelling and Lacan have caught the extreme difference, its irreducibility and heterogeneity with respect to reason, can it be identified with what is disgusting? Isn't disgust something too near to the human being? To be sure, one can maintain the independence and primacy of disgust over taste and attribute to it an asymmetric character that liberates it from any dialectical opposition. But the disgusting is too interwoven and imbued with vitality to constitute a manifestation of the real. Whereby, in the last instance, it seems more the point of arrival of twentieth-century vitalism than the opening of a new post-human and post-organic horizon. The disgusting, in fact, is a life impregnated with death that continues with greater obstinacy than ever its fight against form. It is a desperate and wrathful life, in which a frenzy of destruction rages without end. In the spreading of this fury there is no longer anything homogeneous and different. In fact, the decomposition mingles everything with everything else and, in making everything indistinct and indifferent, homogenizes all that it contaminates.

This is the reason why I believe that the realism of art today cannot be characterized by disgust and abjection alone. If we wish to remain in the proximity of the real, as it was intuited by Schelling and Lacan, we have to move in a direction completely different from vitalism. If it is a question of trauma, it is connected with a state of dispossession and torpor. Schelling uses the expression 'stupor of reason' and, even if he distinguishes it from obtuseness and stupidity,[8] nonetheless, he relates it to a state of stupefaction and astonishment. As far as Lacan is concerned, the real is connected to the 'thing' (*chose*, in German *ding*) understood as mute reality, as something extraneous to meaning.[9] The thing is characterized by the fact that it is impossible for us to imagine it.[10] The idea that art can provide access to the real and to the thing is, in strictly Lacanian terms, untenable. In fact, in his view, art belongs to the realm of the symbolical and not of the real. However, it is not impossible to repeat today, with respect to Lacan's 'thing', what Schopenhauer accomplished in the last century with respect to Kant's 'thing in itself', namely, to attribute to art the faculty of establishing a more direct and essential relation to entities inaccessible to rational thought.

This is precisely what the French philosopher Clément Rosset has tried to do.[11] He introduces the notion of idiocy to point to the accidental and determined character of the real which, on the one hand, is necessarily determined, but this determination does not entail any rationality. In short, it is just any determination which asserts itself anyway with a coercive and even violent character. The term 'idiocy' has to be understood in a double sense: besides the common meaning of stupid and without reason, there is the etymological meaning (from the ancient Greek *idiôtés*) which means simple, particular, unique. The real, therefore, is idiotic precisely because it only exists for itself and is incapable of appearing in any other way than what it is. According to Rosset, the real has a stony and rough character, in short, it is precisely the opposite of the obstinate vitality of disgust. It is incapable of reflecting, duplicating, doubling itself in a specular image. The interpretive activity consists, precisely, in making the real come out of its irreducible singularity and placing it within a process. The production of meaning is an added value to the real by means of an imaginary projection. This interpretative exercise is continuously performed in daily life which is why the experience of the real in its idiocy is something rare. According to Rosset, we grasp the real in its idiocy only in particular conditions, for instance, when we are drunk, or when we have suffered a disappointment in love. There is, however, a third path toward idiocy and this is the path of art. To Schopenauer's and to the Romantic tradition's notion of the artist as genius follows the artist as idiot. What these two figures, which at first appear antithetical, have in common is the claim to grasping the essence of the real beyond all deceitful mediation of language and thought.

The connection between art and idiocy has already been pointed out by Robert Musil in the 1930s, who distinguished between two types of stupidity.[12] There is first of all a simple stupidity, honest and naive, that derives from a certain weakness of reason. It is often close to poetry and art because in the idiot there is something poetic, because of his manner of expression which is extraneous to everyday commonplaces. The second type of stupidity is more interesting because it is strictly related to an unstable and unsuccessful use of intelligence. The claim of today's art to grasp the real without any mediation is close to this type of stupidity. If the essence of stupidity consists in a certain inadequacy with respect to the functionality of life, its exercise seems to Musil to be almost necessarily connected to art. After all, not only is there the occasional stupidity of individuals, but also a constitutional stupidity of the community, whereby it cannot be excluded that the artist idiot, insofar as being an interpreter of social stupidity, is the true organic artist of present society.

3. Splendour of Today's Realism

Extreme realism, however, is not resolved in a purely negative attitude in which the categories of disgust and idiocy prevail. There is also an active force in it that moves in the opposite direction, toward positive or somehow more functional horizons. Two trends have clearly emerged, one oriented toward fashion, the other toward communication.

Extreme realism has generated a substantial amount of images endowed with the strongest emotional impact. They interact with images of fashion, cinema, television, internet, graphics, advertisement, design, making possible a social imaginary characterized by provocation. The search for novelty and effect for its own sake entails a rapid wear and tear and obsolescence of the image, which must be constantly substituted with others possessing greater impact, or with characteristics capable of attracting attention. Thus, art tends to get dissolved in fashion which tends to blunt and extinguish the force of the real, to dissolve its radicalism, to normalize and homogenize everything in a generalized spectacle. The sphere of the real derives from the imaginary, to which Lacan attributes, precisely, a seductive and invalidating power. The imaginary is the realm of illusion, specularity and narcissism. It lacks both the structured and mediated character of the symbolic, and the harsh and inaccessible traumatic character of the real. In order to characterize the imaginary, Lacan introduces the word *captation* which implies, precisely, the twofold action of fascination and imprisonment. To be sure, art is similar to fashion since they share not only the thrill of novelty and challenge, but also the intoxication that ensues from feeling in gear with the spirit of the times. Art, however, is never current in the same sense as fashion is, that is, sociologically prevalent. Already the fact that art is ahead of its time makes it already essentially 'outdated'. Furthermore, what increases this 'outdatedness' is the ambition to escape the wear and tear of time and to constantly arouse surprise and wonder. As a result, from the moment when extreme realism becomes fashionable, it loses its relation to the real and becomes stuck in the snare of the imaginary. With respect to art, fashion is always late, it lives by imitation and recovery.

The second temptation for art today is its dissolution in communication. In fact, the disturbing character of the messages transmitted by the experience of the real is, precisely, what exalts their communicative value. At first, gaining access to wider communicative circuits, such as advertisement and information, may seem attractive for an artistic activity which usually unfolds in rather dull and asphyxiating micro-environments. But in this case too, as for fashion, the imaginary gains the upper hand over the real and the symbolic. According to Lacan, there are two types of discourses that present opposite characteristics. The *parole pleine*, which articulates the symbolic dimension of language, is fundamentally different from *la parole vide*, which articulates the imaginary dimension of language. Only the former is rich in sense (*sens*), the second has only meaning.[13] While the second is easy and fluid, the first is difficult and arduous to articulate. While the second is connected to the phenomena of fictitious identification, aggressiveness and alienation, only the first constitutes a *parole fondante* that deeply transforms whoever speaks and listens. Now, it is clear that extreme art is such because it aspires to this outcome, otherwise nothing would separate it from the artistic trends of the 1980s from which it wants to be strongly disassociated. Furthermore, the dissolution of the work of art in communication would be nothing more than the continuation of subjectivist vitalism. In fact, if there is a difficulty in art, it must not be sought in the subject, in the artist, or in his desire to express himself and communicate, but in the work, in its radical extraneity, in its irreducibility to a single identity, in its essential enigmatic character. Art can never be dissolved in communication because it contains an incommunicable nucleus which is the source of an infinity of interpretations. Under this aspect, it is similar to the real with which it shares the harsh and rocky inconvenience.

The positive character of extreme realism should be looked for in a direction that would save the specificity of art, which is not dissolved in fashion or in communication. Once again Schelling and Lacan point the way. The stupor of reason, of which Schelling speaks, is not only stupefaction and astonishment, but also ecstasy. The state of ecstasy should be considered as the starting point for a positive search that would tear thought away from fixity and muteness.[14] For Schelling this is the road of positive philosophy, that is, of a reason that confronts something outside itself, and that in its turn is placed outside itself. The essential aspect, therefore, is a process of estrangement which is not viewed as an alienation that must be overcome, but as a situation that opens up new horizons.

The notion of alterity is central to the work of Lacan who differentiates a 'great Other' (in capital letter) from a 'small other'.[15] The 'great Other' belongs to the symbolic order and designates a radical alterity irreducible to the projections of the imaginary. Language and the law belong to the sphere of the 'great Other'. More specifically, language is not considered an instrument to express the subjectivity of the I, but an entity endowed with an unconscious dimension, completely other with respect to consciousness. But with regard to the 'small other' Lacan elaborates a more interesting and original theory, especially starting from the moment when, in 1957, he thinks of it under the name of *objet (petit) a*. Starting from 1963, this expression begins to acquire the character of the real. The *objet (petit) a* is the object that by definition can never be reached. It is the *thing* in its mute reality inaccessible both to language and the unconscious.

What the extreme realism of today's art claims to have reached is precisely the *objet (petit) a* of which Lacan speaks. Through it the real no longer irrupts as trauma, but as splendour! Already in the Seminar of 1960–61, Lacan thinks the *objet (petit) a* by attributing to it the characteristics of the Greek word *ágalma* derived from Plato's *Symposium*. Now *ágalma* means, precisely, glory, ornament, gift, image of a divinity and derives from the verb *agállo*, which means to glorify, to exalt. In 1973, Lacan introduces the notion of *semblance* (*semblant*) and defines *objet (petit) a* as a 'semblance of being' and, in stating that love is directed toward a semblance, he places it in relation to *jouissance*.[16]

However, in order to gain access to the splendour of the real a more general and comprehensive approach to the work of Lacan is necessary, that stems from consideration of the object par excellence of his thought: psychosis and its forms. These forms, namely ravings and hallucinations, exhibit the particularly interesting characteristic of imposing on those who are affected as if they belonged to the real. In order to explain this psychic mechanism, Lacan introduces the new notion of 'foreclosure' (*forclusion*). Different from 'removal' (*refoulement*), foreclosure, which is the specific mechanism of psychosis, is not buried in the unconscious, but expelled by the unconscious. Its meanings have not been assimilated in the symbolic order. The foreclosed element, therefore, comes from outside. Lacan completely overturns a common place of psychoanalysis. Mental illness (the gravest of all, psychosis) is not generated from a refusal of the real but, on the contrary, from a lack, by a hole in the symbolic order. In order to emphasize the eccentric and external character of these experiences, Lacan coins the word *extimité* (as opposed to *intimité*) in order to designate a radical exteriority that goes beyond the antithesis between internal and external.

These theoretical materials seem to me of the greatest importance for art and for aesthetics. Those who grasp only the abjection of extreme art without seeing the splendour remain prisoners of a naive idea of the real. In the most meaningful and important works of psychotic realism there is an extreme beauty, for which it is necessary to reinstate a concept of the philosophical tradition now forgotten for more than two centuries, *magnificence*. It is precisely in the eighteenth century that the place of magnificence was taken by the sublime and by luxury. Magnificence, which had found in Aristotle and in Thomas Aquinas great theoretical recognition, now can only undertake a subterranean journey through the paradises and hells of drug addiction and psychosis.[17]

2
Feeling the Difference

1. Aesthetics and Difference

In the title of this chapter merge two different problematics. The first is *feeling* (*sentire*), which a long tradition going back to the eighteenth century links to aesthetics. The second is *difference*, around which originates and develops an important current of contemporary philosophy.

The encounter between aesthetics and the thinking of difference is not at all obvious, or easy. In fact, the quasi totality of aesthetic thinking, in its narrow sense (which identifies and is defined as such) is extraneous to the problematic of difference. It derives either from Kant's *Critique of Judgment* (1968) or from Hegel's *Aesthetics* (1975). From Kant derives the aesthetic of life and the aesthetics of form (the so-called 'Vienna School'), from Hegel, cognitive aesthetics and pragmatic aesthetics. Generally speaking, implicit in aesthetics is the tendency toward ideals of harmony, regularity, and organic unity. Essential to the existence of the aesthetic, at least, is the foreshadowing of an end to conflict, of peace to come, of an irenic moment when suffering and struggle are, if not definitively eliminated, at least temporarily suspended.

On the contrary, the thinking of difference is born with Nietzsche, Freud and Heidegger, from a rejection of aesthetic reconciliation. It moves toward the experience of a conflict greater than dialectical contradiction, toward the exploration of the opposition between terms that are not symmetrically polar with respect to one another. This great philosophical event, which in my view is the most original and the most important of the twentieth century, is known under the notion of 'difference' understood as non-identity, as a dissimilarity greater than the logical concept of diversity and the dialectics of distinction. In other words, access to the experience of difference marks the abandonment both of Aristotle's logic of identity and Hegel's dialectic. No wonder, then, that the thinkers of difference have nothing to do with aesthetics in its narrow sense. In fact, they initiate a new theoretical trend that cannot be reduced to either Kant or Hegel. Their extraneity with respect to the modern aesthetic tradition does not depend at all on exclusive attention to theoretical problems, on disinterest with respect to feeling. In fact, just the contrary is the case. It is precisely from the study of feeling that they were led to put aside post-Kantian and post-Hegelian aesthetics as epigonic and tardy.

In fact, it is doubtful that the notion of 'difference' can be considered a true concept analogous to 'identity', around which revolves Aristotle's logic, or 'contradiction', around which revolves Hegel's dialectic. Rather than within the horizon of pure theoretical speculation, its sphere (or at least its point of departure) is precisely in the impure one of feeling, of unusual and disturbing experiences, irreducible to ambivalent and excessive identities, which has characterized the existence of so many men and women of the twentieth century. The thought of difference has found its inspiration precisely from this type of sensibility that entertains close relations to psychopathological states and mystical ecstasies, drug addiction and perversions, handicaps, minorities, aboriginals, and 'other' cultures. In other words, it is a question of feeling that has nothing to do with exigencies of completeness and reconciliation, which characterize modern aesthetic thinking.

This explains the suspicious attitude toward aesthetics of many founding fathers of the thinking of difference. Nietzsche considers aesthetics an aspect of the naive optimism of tragic experience. Freud believes that aesthetics deals with topics that correspond to a positive state of mind such as the beautiful and the sublime, overlooking those aspects of feeling that are characterized by negative states of mind, such as the uncanny. Heidegger believes that aesthetics is part of Western metaphysics, namely of a thinking characterized by the forgetting of Being. Similarly, the French thinkers of difference (Blanchot, Bataille and Klossowski) inaugurate an approach to literature and art that has nothing to do with aesthetics. Even the Italian philosopher Michelstaedter, who could be considered the most important manifestation of this trend in Italy, is resolutely hostile to Croce's aesthetics.

2. Bliss and Text

It is only recently that the thinking of difference has confronted explicitly aesthetic problematics with Derrida (1978)[18] and Deleuze (1984).[19] My inquiry, however, takes its starting point from a work published previously by Roland Barthes, *The Pleasure of the Text* (1973).[20] It contains an inquiry on feeling that goes well beyond both ancient reflection on pleasure (Plato's pure pleasure or Aristotle's desensitized pleasure), and the modern one linked to eighteenth-century aesthetics and the idea of disinterested pleasure (Kant).

The fundamental crux of Barthes's discourse is in the connection between pleasure and the literary work. But he submits both notions to a deeper transformation, shifting both pleasure and the work of art from the logic of identity to the experience of difference. Beyond pleasure he discovers *bliss* (*jouissance*), beyond the work he discovers the *text*. Bliss is a feeling that goes beyond the distinction between pleasure and pain, but also incorporates what is unpleasant, boring and even painful. It implies the loss of the subject, the disappearance, the *fading*, says Barthes, of personal identity, the abandonment of every cautious and prudent calculation of gratification. Bliss is an excessive experience that irrupts as lightning in individual consciousness striking it and maiming it. The attempt to overcome the hedonistic character of pleasure had already been accomplished by traditional aesthetics through consideration of the tragic and the sublime, but in Barthes's view of bliss there is something more than just the tragic and the sublime. There is the fact that bliss is an erotic experience, strictly connected to sexuality. Barthes repeatedly underlines the perverse character of bliss, namely, its being extraneous to any imaginable finality and launched toward an infinite and insatiable search for the new. But bliss can also be manifested under the aspect of an excessive and maniacal repetition, of a compulsion to repeat that subverts and annuls conventional signification through mimetic and obsessive reiteration, as when by dint of repeating a word we perceive it only as mere sound. Similarly, in Barthes's notion of bliss is also included a series of characteristics that belong, on the one hand to licentiousness, on the other to masochism; on the one hand to the flagrant effervescence of fashion, on the other to the disturbing sexuality of suffering. Thus, bliss seems a mixture of frivolity and death instinct. This is how Barthes liberates aesthetic feeling from that ascetic and sublimated dimension that seemed so essential to it, finding it a place in contemporary experience. Or, as he himself writes, he gave the old category of the aesthetic a slight twist that removed it from its regressive, idealistic background and brought it closer to the body.[21]

A similar strategy is applied by Barthes in the shift from the notion of work to that of *text*. But what does it mean, feeling the text as body? Through what perversion can a work of art become text? The first condition of this shift is its liberation from its ideological aspect. As long as the work is simply considered the bearer of an historical, political, cultural, or psychological meaning, we conceive the work in its identity, as a product endowed with a logical and moral identity. The entry of the work in the problematic of difference breaks up its object-like completeness. That is, it is no longer an object entirely determined by its author such that it cannot be minimally scratched by its fruition. In fact, the reader continues the generative activity of the author in a process without end. This does not mean, however, that the text is dissolved in communication or that pre-eminence is given to the reception of its production. In fact, the opposite is the case. The text is irreducible to a dialogue among subjects, it is somewhat intransitive, atopic and paradoxical. Barthes compares it to cloth not because it covers some hidden meaning, but because it also extends its plot to it. In other words, nothing escapes the text. It is extraneous to the dialectical logic of the dialogue, both to the interface and to the collision of discourses. The text is autonomous and independent of the subjectivity of those who speak and those who listen, those who read and those who write. This is a shift of considerable importance for aesthetics: the passage from 'I feel' to 'one feels'. The whole range of emotions and sensibilities is displaced in the neutral space of the text. If masochism, as we have seen,[22] is the perversion of pleasure, fetishism is the perversion of the work. The fetish is a kind of animation of the inorganic, a coincidence of abstraction and materiality. In fact, the text seems to Barthes something that feels, desires, enjoys.

3. The 'Epoché' and the Neuter

In the philosophy of the 1970s, Roland Barthes seems to me to be the thinker that has most tried to connect intimately sexual feeling to cultural practices within the framework of the problematic of difference, that is, of experiences that are irreducible to traditional aesthetic ideals. Perhaps Luce Irigaray alone has made an equally important contribution, following a different path, but not essentially different. Yet, Barthes's thinking remains locked in a fundamental difficulty as neither his notion of bliss nor of text succeed in emancipating themselves completely from subjectivity. Now bliss falls on the side of hedonism, that is, of the idea of extending the boundaries of pleasure, now on the side of eroticism, that is, of the infinity and insatiability of desire. Now, neither with hedonism nor with eroticism is it possible to move beyond the subject. These are paths that lead us back to the side of the aesthetic rather than leading us forward to the path of difference. A similar phenomenon occurs with regard to the text. Barthes's polemic against the institutionalization of the text, that is, against the specialism of theorists and critics, leads him to emphasize the personal, fragmentary and incidental character of his writing, distancing it from philosophy. This tendency, already self-evident in the autobiographical work *Roland Barthes by Roland Barthes* (1975), intensifies in the later writings, for instance in the posthumous *Incidents* (1987).

Nonetheless there are elements in *The Pleasure of the Text* that run counter to the subject toward a radicalization of the feeling of difference, namely, *the critique of desire* and the idea of the text as *thing*. According to Barthes, the infinity of desire, which has seemed to many a guarantee of its philosophical character, in fact only generalizes the delusion. Difference is not absence! As long as I think of the alternative to Western metaphysics in terms of lack, I remain prisoner of a mode of thinking opposites (already foreseen in Aristotle's metaphysics) which is lesser not greater than dialectical contradiction. The second idea of the text as thing, although not formulated explicitly, seems to me to be contained in Barthes's distinction between representation and symbolization (*figuration*). While the text as object falls entirely within the sphere of metaphysics and traditional aesthetics, the text as thing is within the horizon opened up by the notion of difference. Barthes's *Camera lucida; Reflections on Photography* (1980) can be viewed as a development of this idea.

There are however two other elements that can bring greater clarity and simplicity to these complex and difficult questions: the experience of the *epoché* and the notion of *neuter*. Barthes refers to both but they are never given a major place in his work[23] and yet only through them can sexual feeling and the thinking of difference be united inseparably. Only through them sexuality and philosophy reveal that they essentially belong together. As we have seen, the issue around which Barthes's thinking revolves can be formulated in these terms: how is it possible to go beyond subjective feeling? How is it possible to remove the sphere of sensation, affection, and emotionality from the tyranny of 'I feel'? How do we arrive at the impersonal 'one feels'? How can one discover an other, different, extraneous territory of feeling where the 'I' and the 'you' finally give way to an experience independent of the 'self'? Western philosophy has known the answer ever since the age of the ancient philosophers. In fact the Sceptics and the Stoics were the first to introduce the experience of the *epoché*, a suspension of passions and subjective affections. These, according to the Stoics, could be reduced to four: pleasure, pain, desire, fear. The suspension, however, must not be understood as total insensibility but as a non-participating participation, a sober intoxication, a feeling with distance. In other words, as if I were not the one to feel, or, better, as if I were a 'thing that feels' in an impersonal way and without boundaries, without being aware where my corporeal identity ends and the body of another physical entity begins. It is a question, in short, of a feeling that explodes the separation between self and non-self, internal and external, human beings and things.

It seems clear to me that this type of feeling cannot be defined in terms of hedonistic categories. It is a feeling beyond pleasure and pain but also beyond bliss because it refers to an experience which is too spiritual, like ecstasy, while what is essential here is the reference to the mode of being of the thing, to which abstraction can be relevant but not spirituality. Similarly inadequate it seems to me are erotic categories. Erotic desire implies the idea of holding out toward something and, thus, the experience of a loss, while here is a question of availability which, however, is not a true metaphysical presence. There is in the idea of availability a more opaque aspect that goes, on the one hand, toward virtuality, on the other, toward exchange value and money. Finally, this feeling, which is resolutely extraneous to any purpose, both practical and cognitive, cannot even be considered aesthetic, since it has nothing to do with the desexualized sublimation of aesthetic experience.

Now, even though *epoché* is a bimillenarian notion, Western philosophy has made a modest and timid use of it. We had the cognitive *epoché* of the ancient Sceptics and of modern phenomenology, the moral *epoché* of the Stoics and Neo-Stoics, but there has never been a sexual *epoché* because in sexuality the rush toward orgasm has always seemed implicit, without any possibility of suspension, except a tactical one directed to prolonging pleasure or increasing desire. Sexuality has always been seen as functional with respect to the gratification or satisfaction of a need, and almost never within a philosophical perspective of research and exploration of unknown territories.

Sexual *epoché* leads us toward a sexuality beyond pleasure and desire, no longer finalized with respect to orgasm but suspended in abstract and infinite excitement, without concern for beauty, age, and, generally, form. In contrast to vitalistic sexuality, based on the distinction between the sexes, and permeated by hedonism and eroticism, we could define an inorganic sexuality moved by the '*sex appeal of the inorganic*'.[24] Here the notion of *neuter* plays a pivotal role. Inorganic sexuality, in fact, is beyond the distinction between masculine and feminine. The neuter, however, must not be understood as an harmonic recomposition of masculine and feminine, as a dialectical synthesis of opposites. Just the opposite, in fact, the neuter is the point of arrival of the experience of difference and, therefore, irreducible to unity and identity. In other words, a neuter sexuality is neither sublimated nor neutralized. By abolishing the division between masculine and feminine, it establishes a multiplicity of other divisions giving way to infinite sexual virtualities. In fact, this is the essence of sexuality, namely, cutting (*secare*), establishing divisions, making differences. But in order to move on this path, it is necessary, first of all, to free oneself from the false difference between masculine and feminine whose purpose is to assert identities and to sanction discriminations.

4. Two Versions of the 'Sex Appeal' of the Inorganic

The *sex appeal* of the inorganic can be thought in many ways. If by 'inorganic' we understand the natural mineral world, neuter sexuality can be nourished by the excitement created by the inversion through which human beings are perceived as things and, on the contrary, things are seen as living beings. I would consider this phenomenon as the 'Egyptian version' of the *sex appeal* of the inorganic, on the authority of a passage from Hegel who attributes to that ancient people the reification of humans accompanied by a

sensitization of the environment.[25] In the so-called 'Egyptomania',
which in past centuries has constituted a very important cultural
trend, is implicit a sexual excitement that is nourished by fetishistic,
sadomasochistic and necrophiliac aspects, of which *bondage*, con-
jured up by the mummies, is the most well-known and self-evident.
Furthermore, if we think that Egypt was also the country par excellence of ideographic writing, we get the connection between sexuality
and textuality that Roland Barthes examines in his work.

Another version of the *sex appeal* of the inorganic is the one that
refers to electronic and cybernetic technology. It could be defined as
the '*cyberpunk* version' of the *sex appeal* of the inorganic. Inspired by
a will to overcome natural limitations, it asks about the feeling of
the *cyborg*, namely, the science fiction character whose organs are
replaced with artificial devices (for example, telecameras instead of
eyes, antennae instead of ears). This perspective opens up an horizon of the 'post-human' or 'post-organic' type, where the shift of the
centre of sensibility from man to *computer* is key. Thus the problematic of 'artificial feeling' is born, whose essential character is to
be experimental. The most interesting aspect of this orientation is
not to provide a substitute for real sexuality (as in *cybersex*), but to
develop neuter sexuality which is anchored on the philosophical
experience of the *epoché*. Through it, I perceive my body as a thing,
for instance, as a suit, or as an electronic device. In other words,
'artificial feeling' is not a replica of natural feeling, but the access
to a different feeling, a different, neuter sexuality, no longer centred
on the identity of consciousness but overflowing and excessive. I become an extraneous body, I de-subjectivize experience, I expel from
me my organs and my feeling and localize them in something
external. I become the difference.

5. Psychotic Realism

Beside the 'Egyptian' and 'Cyberpunk' versions there is a third
version of the *sex appeal* of the inorganic that seems to me to be
more disquieting than the first two. If one of the essential characters
of inorganic sexuality is that of abolishing the borders between the I
and the not-I, the proper and the extraneous, the self and not-self, it
reveals itself to be very close to madness, in fact, close to that
particular type of madness that has been defined as *psychosis*. In fact,
a characteristic of psychosis is the identification with the outside

world: I am fascinated with exteriority. I become what I see, feel, touch. In fact, it is as if the surface of my body identifies with the surface of the external world. Most often this tendency assumes a cosmic aspect, for instance, in a classic text of the beginning of the twentieth century, Daniel Paul Schreber's *Memoirs of my Nervous Illness*, where he describes the process through which the loss of identity coincides with a willingness to become anything, to be everything. Schreber feels that his body does not belong to him any longer. It can become the virgin Mary or a prostitute, a national saint or a woman of the North, a Jesuit novice or a young Alsatian woman that struggles in the arms of a French officer who wants to rape her, or still prince Mogol, or something abstract such as the cause of atmospheric phenomena. This experience is connected to an excitement that soon becomes the only reason for living.[26]

The worrying aspect of this phenomenon is its spreading to contemporary aesthetic sensibility. In the more advanced artistic trends, the traditional structure of separation between art and the real seems collapsed definitively. A new species of 'psychotic realism' is born that collapses any mediation. Art loses its distance with respect to reality and acquires a physical and material character that it never had before: music is sound, theatre is action, the figurative arts have a consistency both visual, tactile and conceptual. They are no longer imitations of reality but reality *tout court*, no longer mediated by aesthetic experience. They are extensions of the human faculty that no longer have to account to a subject because this is completely dissolved in a radical exteriority.

This artistic trend oriented toward an always more crude realism seems to have had origins in the nineteenth century. Present psychotic realism could be taken to be the point of arrival of naturalism, to which the philosopher Wilhelm Dilthey attributed the claim of grasping reality in an immediate manner, without stopping even before the physiological and the bestial.[27] For Dilthey naturalism marks the end of a conception of life and art that began in Europe in the Renaissance. Yielding to mere empirical factuality, inherent in the poetics of reproduction of reality, represents the liquidation of the European philosophical and artistic heritage. Similarly, many years later, the philosopher György Lukács chose naturalism as the target of his aesthetics attributing to it the same characteristics, namely, confusion between art and life, dogmatic mirroring of reality, apologia of the existent.[28]

Since the era of Dilthey and Lukács, naturalism has further radicalized its characteristics. Precisely during the 1990s, it found a new and exuberant development becoming the most emergent literary and artistic trend. For example, the novels of Bret Easton Ellis[29] and James Ellroy[30] constitute impressive manifestations of literature's attempt to perfectly adhere to the most cruel criminal realities.

Psychotic realism also revealed itself in the figurative arts, precisely at the beginning of the 1990s, through an entire series of important international exhibitions[31] (*Post human, Hors limites, L'art et la vie* and *Sensation*), as well as trendy magazines (*Virus* in Milan, and *Bloc Notes* in Paris). Another manifestation of this trend is represented by the so-called artists of the 'extreme body' (the Spanish Marcel. Lí Antunez Roca, the French Orlan, the Australian Stelarc). These artists engage their bodies in dangerous experiments, directed toward the discovery of new forms of perception and feeling.[32]

In movies and videos, the poetics of reproduction of a real phenomenon caught in the moment in which it occurs has been brought to its extreme consequences. After all, this is an ambition that the cinema has had since its origins with the Brothers Lumière and which has characterized the entire problematic of the documentary from Vertov to the *cinéma-verité* of the 1960s, to visual anthropology. In the 1990s this problematic was rethought in a more radical way in some of the films of Wim Wenders and Derek Jarman which constitute an important reflection on the way in which the relation between image and reality is articulated today.

And yet it is precisely in the cinema that psychotic realism shows its limitations, for two reasons. In the first place, it is difficult to consider the *business* of brute reproduction of the most crude realities (sex, extreme violence, death) a manifestation of difference. One can hardly deny that *gore, splatter, trash* constitute a banal version of experiences that are actually known by only a few. The second reason, which seems to me to be more crucial, is that there is no longer any guarantee that what we are witnessing is true. In fact, the possibility exists of manipulating any visual document electronically. Thus, the reality effect that constituted the main cause of excitement of this type of product is lacking. We could say that what has done away with naturalism and *cinéma-verité* is not morality but electronics.

The notion of *abjection*, elaborated by Julia Kristeva,[33] seems to provide a very acute interpretation of these phenomena. Its essential character is precisely the collapse of the borderline between internal and external, inside and outside. Kristeva's analysis moves on three levels: psychoanalytical, religious, and literary. According to her, for those who recognize themselves in abjection, the emission of internal contents such as urine, blood, sperm, excrements becomes the only object of sexual interest because it overflows from its subjective identity, from its 'internal hole', and, therefore, guarantees it indirectly. Differently from sacrificial religions which tend to exclude any mixing between internal purity and external impurity, Christianity marks a turning point of great fundamental importance because it interiorizes and spiritualizes impurity. Thus, in a certain sense, it introduces abjection in culture and in literature.

Nonetheless, I cannot accept abjection as a solution. We must not forget that the essential aspect of the thinking of difference lies in the effort to map an alternative path to Western onto-theological categories. And it is not difficult to detect in abjection a manifestation of absolute hostility toward the world and the human body, considered as evil. In other words, feeling the difference cannot mean insisting on the most crude and repellent facts. We would end up by falling into the very thing we were trying to emerge from: spiritualism, anti-worldly fanaticism, the most repressive tradition. The poetics of *trash* and abjection restore indirectly precisely what the thinking of difference is fighting against. If the human being is just garbage, this means that the only one to shine is the transcendental!

6. Toward the Extremely Beautiful

The aesthetics of difference has to look elsewhere in the direction of notions of *neuter* and *epoché*. Once again, it is Barthes who can point the way. First of all *neuter* does not mean *neutralization*. In a brief text based on the course he gave at the Collège de France, Barthes explains that *neuter* does not mean the abolition of conflictual data of discourse but, on the contrary, their preservation and indefinite proliferation. Barthes's aim was to show that 'neuter did not correspond necessarily to the flat image, and depreciated as a result, that Doxa has, but could constitute a strong, active, value.'[34] In other words, I access the *neuter* when I realize that the opposition put up by current opinion (for instance, between masculine and feminine) is inadequate to describe my experience, not because a possibility of reconciliation has emerged between the two terms, but because a third term has intervened (for instance, the feeling of inorganic sexuality), that is, different with respect to the way in which sexuality has been thought so far. Thus *epoché* does not mean insensitivity or flattening of the facts but simply not being involved in a false conflict (for instance, between masculine and feminine). Barthes, in describing the feeling of love, left out of consideration the sex of the object at issue and spoke more generally of an *other* (*autre*).[35] Against the intimation of the contemporary world to choose between two contestants, between two factions, between two possibilities arbitrarily posited as antinomies, Barthes vindicates 'the right to suspend one's judgement',[36] by referring expressly to the ancient Sceptics.

To conclude, psychotic realism remains within the sphere of alternative experiences only to the extent to which it understands the real as what exceeds, by definition, banality, the *status quo*, facts. It is mystifying to present ugliness as a type of the beautiful and abjection as an experience to be recommended. It would be like taking coarseness as sincerity or villainy as transparence. Barthes teaches that difference, the text of life, life as text, lives in the *more*.[37] 'That is why it is a goddess, a figure that can be invoked, a mode of intercession.'

3
Warhol and the Postmodern

1. *The Postmodern Dissensus*

'After the modern there is the postmodern, but what is there *after* the postmodern?' I do not believe that Andy Warhol ever said or wrote this phrase, but it seems to me to be a good starting point to ask about his relation with a trend that defines itself and is determined on the basis of its own opposition to something that preceded it in time, namely the modern.

From the beginning, in fact, the postmodern is the victim of an attitude which recognizes, on the one hand, the importance and unavoidability of what preceded it, on the other, its own essence depends on its opposition to it. The postmodern asserts *at the same time* the necessity of the continuation of the modern and its abolition. This operation is realized according to a logic which is not the dynamic one of Hegelian dialectic, in which the overcoming (*aufhebung*) actually opens a new horizon with respect to the past, but is the static one of those who immobilize a conflict through the determination of opposite characteristics. This is precisely the kind of analysis conducted by Ihab Hassan, one of the first theorists of postmodernism, with his famous table with two columns where in one are placed the key notions of modernism and in the other the specularly opposite ones of postmodernism. Some of these dichotomies (as those between project and case, presence and absence, type and mutant, semantics and rhetoric, metaphysics and irony) have become famous and have found numerous applications and variations. At the end of the postmodern parabola, David Harvey offers once again a table where Hassan's formulations, mostly philosophical and literary, are integrated with economic and political ones, such as: capital accumulation, entrepreneurship, collective consumption, symbolic capital, industrialization, de-industrialization, and so on.[38]

These tables in their schemata are very useful to understand the contents of postmodern poetics. However, it is even more important to ask why the form of the dichotomy table holds such an essential relation to postmodernism. In fact, it could not survive without the support of modernism, from which it derives its reason for being. The schemata of the opposition table reveals the essential aspect of the postmodern, that is, its being blocked in an oppositive duplication. This opposition does not take shape as a new dialectical contradiction from which something new is born. In fact, the postmodern abandons the emphasis placed by modernity on novelty, originality, the avant-garde. This opposition cannot even be thought as a polarity in which the two terms are symmetrical. The postmodern is not at the same level as the modern because it comes *after* the modern, even if this posterity must not be thought necessarily as historical. From the dialectical point of view, the postmodern appears as a parasite of the modern. From the point of view of the polarity, it appears as a surrogate of the modern. Viewed from the outside, the postmodern seems opposed to the modern even if it seems incapable of being really such. Its opposition seems over-ambitious, its antagonism bound to remain subordinate. It is as if it lacked the courage and the dignity of the struggle, as if it were not capable of being the real enemy of the modern.

This problematic is at the centre of the reflection of Jean-François Lyotard, the French philosopher and author of *The Postmodern Condition*.[39] In fact, in his view, the postmodern is part of the modern. They are both removed from the past and regard it as suspect, but while the former remains a prisoner of those ideals of emancipation of humanity, which turned out to be pious illusions, the latter is removed from facile consolations and proceeds to a kind of re-elaboration not unlike that of psychoanalytical analysis. That is why the postmodern must be understood not so much as the mere repetition of the modern but as its 'anamnesis',[40] its disenchanted and unbiased exam, its critical and demystified critique.

The entire work of Andy Warhol stands on this tension between modern and postmodern. Its point of departure is the image of modern information such as we find in newspapers, television or advertisement. This image conveys the modern myths of beauty (Marilyn Monroe) well-being (Coke), power (Mao Tse Tung), wealth (Gianni Agnelli), success (Elvis Presley) and so on. Warhol submits the image to a process of transformation that removes it from 'directly competitive and competing' *business* so to speak, and places it in *another business*, that of art. The business of art, however, is not really an alternative with respect to the other, but constitutes, precisely, a kind of opposite duplicate of the first. *Art business* constitutes a kind of particular *business* but is always a 'production' and not really creative doing. While the latter implies the presence of a creative subject, the former has 'nothing personal'. Hence, Warhol concludes that whereas the artist can also not care about what is written about him, the director of an artistic enterprise must hold the press in the greatest consideration to determine whether it is possible to make use of it somehow. In short, self-promotion is an autonomous mechanism which does not proceed all by itself, but entails the greatest commitment. From this perspective, Andy Warhol's *The Philosophy of Andy Warhol*[41] constitutes a very interesting guide to postmodern cultural work by showing that artistic *management* is not any less difficult than the generally commercial one. But the work is also a type of *vademecum* on how to live, where one can find practical advice derived from ancient wisdom, from the Stoics in fact, such as never complain about a situation as long as you are in it, or be completely detached from your emotions, as if you were living in a movie.

2. Warhol's Cynicism

This suspension of the emotional dimension, however, is a lot more than a personal trait of Warhol. It can be considered a characteristic of postmodern sensibility which has been interpreted in many ways: now as irony, now as deliberate superficiality.[42] According to Warhol, it goes back to the 1960s which is that period, precisely, in which people forgot the emotional aspect of life and has no longer remembered it since. The German writer Peter Sloterdijk has focused his attention on this problematic. In his view, the postmodern experience qualifies above all for its cynicism. He differentiates between present cynicism, in which critical awareness of contemporary society supports unprincipled and dishonest actions, and the ancient cynicism of Diogenes and his followers in which the critique of social conventions was inseparable from a coherent practice of refusal to compromise. Sloterdijk thus shows how the annulment of passions can lead to opposite results. In the ancient world it led to freedom and individual autonomy; in postmodern-ism, instead, to a conformism associated to the basest actions. Postmodern feeling, therefore, seems paralyzed by a conflict between a knowing more than ever lucid and profound, and a deliberate immorality without restraint or decency.

A similar conflict is at work in Warhol, who has often been taken as an example of cynicism without equal. His vision of con-temporary society is without ideological veils and is closer to the counter-culture of the 1960s. However, this does not lead him to openly refute capitalism, *The American Way of Life*, the society of the spectacle, but to establish with these realities a relation of burlesque rivalry, of oppositive duplication, which can be compared to the relation of transvestites to femininity. Now, who is a transvestite? An enemy or a friend of women? It seems to me that he is, rather, someone who introduces a strategic play different not only from the traditional logic of political conflict (which considers the enemy as an *alter ego*), but also from unfair competition (that wants to reach the same objective as the competitor by any means). Now, Warhol does not believe at all that art can represent a real opposition to bourgeois society, or that it can provide a product that even partially could take the place of the cultural industry. The images, the schemes, the modalities are those of advanced capitalism and there are no others. The only possible artistic action consists in producing something that takes up their forms in an exaggerated manner displacing them in another contest which is at the same time similar and different with respect to the point of departure. As the trans-vestite is both superfeminine and antifeminine, so Warhol's art is both supercapitalist and anticapitalist. On the one hand, Warhol's art is a supercommodity whose economic value is hyperbolically disproportionate with respect to the value of the materials employed and to the work done to realize it; on the other hand, the fact that it utilizes the same materials and the same forms of the products of capitalistic industry ridicules the latter on its own ground, namely, that of speculation and exploitation. Thus, on the one hand, the transvestite exalts femininity beyond any limit, on the other it reproaches the woman, implicitly, for not being sufficiently femi-nine. In either case, only one discourse is possible: that of femininity for the transvestite, that of modern capitalism for postmodern art. At the same time, however, they tend to level an accusation to femininity and capitalist society. Warhol is after all deeply fascinated by transvestitism. In his film, *Women in Revolt*, the three main female characters are played by three transvestites!

In contrast to what was happening in the era of counter-culture, which characterized the 1960s and part of the 1970s, postmodernism knows very well that there is no tribunal before which they can lay their charge. In fact, if there are judges, then he is the accused! He is under no condition to prove that he was wronged, on the contrary, he must defend himself from charges of fraud. Lyotard has devoted his most important work, *The Differend*, to analyse the situation in which the victim cannot demonstrate that he has been wronged.[43] The *dissensus* (différend) consists precisely in the fact that the actor is deprived of the means to argue his case and thus becomes a victim. In fact, a quarrel is transformed into an insoluble dissensus when there is no single rule of judgement that can be applied to both parties. In the suit that the postmodern brings against the modern, the charge of the former ends in a paradox. To introduce repetition and mimesis as something new, that breaks the logic of innovation typical of modernity, means falling into a logical antinomy that Lyotard defines, precisely, with the technical term *dissensus*. By extending the paradoxical logic of the dissensus to the question of postmodernism, I would like to offer this alternative. Either the postmodern actually introduces something new and then it continues the logic of the modern and, thus, cannot charge it with anything; or the postmodern does not introduce anything new and, thus, continues the modern and is its accomplice. In both cases, the postmodern is an imposture, in the first case because it does not say what it actually is (namely, modern), in the latter case, because it says what it is not (namely, new). Nor can we justify the first horn of the dilemma as a form of 'honest dissimulation' because the postmodern displays an aggressive and derogative attitude towards the modern!

It may seem a provocation to present Warhol as a victim who finds it impossible to defend his own cause, especially when he represents the example par excellence of economic and worldly success in the field of culture! However, there is a wretched side to Warhol that he has not concealed. The pages of his *Philosophy of Andy Warhol* that tell of his fears that he may miss the great worldly 'Event' in Rome, the new capital of celebrities, where a great number of *stars* are gathered, throws a pathetic and pitiful light on his artistic projects. He seems to us a poor bloke who runs after the powerful of the earth to be photographed with them. To be sure, this behaviour is functional with respect to his intention to sell their manipulated photo-IDs for their weight in gold, but his behaviour is a thousand miles distant from the style of the true *dandies*, free spirits such as Brummel and Baudelaire.

3. Sexuality, Suffering and Genetics

Warhol's postmodern transvestitism goes hand in hand with a de-sexualization and a de-legitimization of art. It obscures the difference and alterity of both sexual and artistic experience. Both are diluted in a conciliatory aestheticism, in a nerve-racking cosmetics that blunts sensibility and affectivity. Warhol is far from the tensions that animated the modernist avant-garde and yet he is incapable of jumping out of that dialectic of unacknowledgment and recognition that characterizes the movement of modern art. New art, he remarks, is never new when it is realized. It only becomes new when ten years have elapsed from its production. Once again he is a prisoner of a dissensus, an antinomy he cannot resolve.

The cultural and artistic events that follow postmodernism move toward a resexualization and a revaluation of art. They mark an irruption of the real in art. It is the hard nut of the real, its most traumatic and disturbing core that forces itself on the attention of artists. Postmodernism played an anaesthetizing and narcotic role with respect to sex and suffering. Now it is the turn of sexual difference and the ineliminability of suffering to vindicate their rights. For instance, the works of Barbara Kruger, Cindy Sherman or Jane Sterback move precisely in this direction. After all, Warhol collided prematurely and dramatically with this reality when Valerie Solanas, the founder of SCUM (Society for Cutting Up Men), made an attempt on his life in 1968. The idea that a re-legitimization of art can pass through the experience of corporal pain is inherent in the so-called *performance* of the 'extreme body'. Through them a problematic opens up that has nothing to do with the postmodern.

Sexuality and suffering, instead, constitute great challenges for postmodernism. But they are not the only ones. A third challenge to postmodernism comes from multiculturalism which reproaches it as a complicity with the politics of an imperialistic culture. Warhol lends himself particularly to this accusation, precisely because he attributes to the American cultural industry a hegemonic function

on a world scale. The circumstances of his collaboration with the
painter of Caribbean origin, Jean-Michel Basquiat, that began in
1983 and which inspired the film *Basquiat* of Julian Schnabel
(where the role of Warhol is eminently played by David Bowie),
deserve a more careful study. How Basquiat's neo-primitivism can
be reconciled with postmodernism is a very interesting question.
In fact, on the one hand, it seems to be the bearer of vitalist
aspirations, deeply rooted in the historical avant-garde, which are
an alternative to postmodern frigidity; on the other hand, neo-
primitivism too can be seen as a repetition of an important aspect of
modern sensibility. The collaboration between Warhol and Basquiat
gives way, too, to an insoluble dilemma, which one could only
resolve with a critique of modernity much more explicit and radical
than the one attempted by postmodernism.

The basic problem is that of a possible convergence between
Western tradition and extra-European cultures, but this accord
depends on a type of anthropological approach to the ancient
origins of Western civilization that would shed light on its deep
affinities with the cultures of Africa and Asia. Now, even though
much progress has been made by the history of religions and by the
anthropology of the classical world (and by ethnophilosophy), one
still cannot understand how a *neo-ancient* (but not neo-classic) trend
can assert itself in the field of the figurative arts, which could vehicle
an alternative sensibility to the prevailing one in Western cultural
industry. Perhaps from the development of *rock* music come the
most interesting suggestions on this point. It seems to me important
to note that Basquiat was above all a musician! In fact, in mixing *world music* and *rock*, we can see a neo-ancient solution to the
postmodern conflict.

To conclude, there are three thorns in the side of the postmodern: sexuality, suffering, and genetics. All three elements relate
to the body understood as something given, on which one can act
but one cannot leave out of consideration. Postmodernism clashes
with physiology. While it placed stress on simulation and synthesis,
the physiological turn focuses on the 'being thing' in all its non-
conceptuality and incomprehensibility. We live by now in a cultural
context that is no longer postmodern.

A question of capital importance now emerges with respect to
which postmodernism had an attitude of denial (*Verleugnung*):
value. In fact, on the one hand, postmodernism denies the reality of

a value difference among cultural products, on the other it becomes aware of the existence of a remainder, a plus and minus, something that we do not succeed in cancelling with an arithmetic operation whose result is zero. As we know, Freud elaborated the notion of denial on the basis of the privileged example of fetishism. And for Baudrillard the category of fetishism seems to be the category most relevant to explain the phenomenon of Warhol.[44] With him, superstition in the value of art has taken the place of faith.

Contrary to Leonardo da Vinci, who persuaded his patrons that the time spent in thinking was worthwhile, Warhol asserts that he wants to be paid only for the time that he produces. Thus, by attributing to production time a hyperbolic value, he practically annuls his importance in the determination of the economic value of his works! What counts is the immediate idea, the concept, which is precisely fetishized in the work

All this could lead to Joseph Kosuth's conclusion that conceptual art follows philosophy. In this regard, in fact, Lyotard observes, melancholically, that in a universe where success is gaining time, thinking has only one incorrigible flaw, it makes you lose it![45] In the postmodern situation what counts is the promotional presentation of the book which precedes it and dissolves it, transforming it very rapidly in a remainder! How can one remove philosophy from this condition that places it in a situation of humiliation and disheartenment with respect to art? Through an immoderate production and an insane showing of oneself everywhere in the *media*? Through the production of philosophical 'art books'? Through the invention of a philosophical video and cinema?

Lyotard's answer is another. The value of a work of art or thought depends on its capacity to generate a future. In one word, it bets on *making it* (*arriver*)! This term includes the event, the getting there, the arriving at destination. But is there still a possibility of *making it* for those who preferred to celebrate Mao instead of Marcuse, Liz Taylor instead of Lyotard?

4
Toward a Philosophical Cinema

1. A Visual Philosophy?

The question of the relation between cinema and philosophy underlies the entire history of the cinema. Since its origins one has had
to pose questions of a philosophical nature such as the relation
between reality and its reproduction, the cognitive potentiality of
the cinematographic medium, the representation of abstract ideas,
the spectacular character of the collective imaginary, the contribution made by the cinema to the knowledge of emotions, behaviours
and experiences. To the origins of the cinema goes back the quarrel
over the essential narrative or documentary character of cinema.
Although the first thesis has enjoyed, besides popular favour, also
the support of a few theoretical analyses, it seems to me hardly
challengeable that an approach oriented toward the production of
philosophical cinema would find its point of departure in the study
of the documentary. Even without claiming any superiority of the
mimetic over diegetic cinema, it seems to me inevitable that problems encountered by those who want to espouse philosophical
experience with the cinema exhibit some affinity with problems
confronted by scientific cinema (historical, anthropological, sociological, archaeological, psychoanalytical, and so on). Although it is
difficult to define a documentary, philosophical cinema meets the
documentary's intention at least 'in attesting to the existence of
something anterior to itself, or independent of itself; something
that could be approached with cognitive instruments different from
those of the cinema'.[46] However, the questions of those who starting from philosophy move closer to cinema in a creative way are
quite the opposite. They ask whether it is possible to really make a
philosophical film, that is, a film that would not be merely didactic,
hortatory, or propagandistic, but that could be considered a rela-
tively autonomous philosophical work. Is philosophical experience
something that can only be articulated through language, or is it

possible to establish correlations between language and the world of images, sounds, actions, places? Beside linguistic thinking, is there a thinking which is visual, sonorous, ritual, spatial? Or 'do words have a sense [ ] that images do not have,' as it was stated provokingly with regard to the work of Chris Marker?[47] Can cinema create a total philosophical work that would comprehend and coordinate writing, vision, listening, event and spatiality?

These questions would be idle if they did not arise out of the confluence of two problematics of which one is philosophical and the other cinematographic. On the one hand, philosophy resorts more often than not to descriptive processes. For instance, Gilles Deleuze's book on the Baroque, *The Fold*, is so rich with metaphors that it seems to invite a transposition into film.[48] On the other hand, cinema too, in its most reflexive and self-aware moment, has doubts on the autonomy of the image and invites the intervention of a language that has a different status from that of everyday, for instance, Wim Wenders's *Lisbon Story* (1994), whose main issue is precisely the experience of the inadequacy of the image.

2. *The Library of Images Not Seen*

Wenders's film, initially a documentary on Lisbon, and also his contribution to the celebrations for the centennial of the cinema, constitutes a kind of propaedeutic to visual philosophy. His point of departure is the recognition of the crisis of the cinematographic image. Displaced by video, which by now combines an extreme flexibility with highly technical quality, the cinema has lost the confidence of being able to create a visual product endowed with a status completely different from what the novelty of television, *home video*, and advertisement have in common. We are flooded by an avalanche of garbage-images that impair and blunt our ability for discrimination, wonder and admiration. We have become 'video-idiots.' Images are 'for sale'. What is the point of doing a documentary on Lisbon if the visual results are not perceived as something fundamentally different from those obtained by some kids with a video camera? However, the cinema is not only video but audio too. Now the charm of *Lisbon Story* rests precisely on listening. Not on listening to a script. The plot is reduced to a minimum. The reduction of the importance of the diegetic aspect is the point of departure of visual philosophy. Wenders's film derives its substance from *another* word which is that of history, poetry, song, and philosophy. But history, above all! With the European Union, Lisbon is transformed from a marginal city into a big city, from a secondary place to distinctive place par excellence. Then poetry. Very shrewdly, the main character reads long passages from the work of Pessoa. In fact, in the movie there is no comparable image. It is significative that Wenders turns to poetry rather than to painting for help! Then song, the music, the sound landscape. What would the movie be without the performance of 'I Madredeus'? Let us also ask: what would change if 'I Madredeus' were an invention, instead of being real? And if we were to listen to their music without ever seeing them in person? And what if the main character of the movie, the phonic Philip Winter, really existed? And what if he were the author of the soundtrack instead of being the actor? These questions help us understand on which combination of reality and fictional effects a cultural product must rely nowadays in order to generate some kind of interest. More essentially, they also help us understand that no work can pretend to remain closed in its own form. It overflows on every side and invites a series of extrinsic integrations that alter the perception that we have of it. Finally, philosophy. When the great Portuguese director Manoel de Oliveira appears on the screen to explain to us that the film guarantees the existence of a moment that will soon fade, we have the impression that after a hundred years of film history the documentary is finally prevailing over narrative.

But Wenders's film has an even greater ambition. It is already fully formulated by the phrase that hovers over the wall of the room where the main character lives: 'Ah, not to be all the people of all the places!' (*Ah não ser eu toda a gente e toda a parte!*) This exclamatory phrase can be interpreted in two ways. On the one hand, it manifests an essential characteristic of psychosis, on the other, it reveals a cosmic attitude with respect to the world. The rejection of individual identity, the becoming nothing and nobody in order to become everything, mimesis brought to complete identification with the feeling of the other, represent powerful cognitive devices of the world and reality, beside being intoxicating, exciting, even dizzying experiences, which, on the one hand, allow a deep comprehension of disquieting aspects of madness, and on the other, free one from the sadness and the despair of being prisoners of an identity. But beyond the psychotic and cosmic effect of wanting to be everything, there is a third one, strictly cinematographic, that constitutes the very plot of the movie. In fact, the movie tells the story of a director who while making a film on Lisbon is caught by a series of doubts and uncertainties on the status of the cinematographic image as representation of reality. He undertakes, therefore, an experiment that consists in taking images of the city without looking in the camera, at the same time that he lets himself go to an 'urban drifting' without return. The experiment is based on the presupposition that these images have a more essential relation with what they represent: 'An image not seen is in perfect unison with the world!' But they cannot even be seen by the spectator! Therefore, they constitute a testimony, a monument, a fetish which is 'thing' by the same right as what is represented. Between the city and the image there is no longer representation or mimesis, but total identification. Both the cameraman and the spectator disappear leaving the object and its image to unite without being any longer contaminated by the human glance. The only 'true' documentary on Lisbon would be 'the library of images not seen,' a radical alternative to the garbage-images of the video-idiots of our time.

3. *Is it Fair to Punish Horizontal Collaborators?*

Are there images that merit consideration for their autonomous conceptual meaning? Guy Debord, the author of *The Society of the Spectacle* (1967) and the film of the same name (1973), has his doubts. In fact, his film is substantially an illustration of the book. While a voice reads passages from the book, on the screen are projected excerpts from the films of John Ford, Nicholas Ray, Joseph von Sternberg, Orson Welles, as well as from a number of unknown directors, mixed to images of newsreel and advertisement. Therefore, the film is essentially a work of montage, whose common thread is constituted by theoretical language.[49] This raises a fundamental problem. If we were to substitute the chosen images with others taken from other films, would the results be the same? And even when Debord employs images from documentaries, they count more for their symbolic value than for their visual specificity. For instance, if instead of the Beatles we used the Rolling Stones, if instead of Marilyn Monroe we saw Brigitte Bardot, nothing would change. Therefore, from the film we get the impression of the absolute primacy of theoretical language, regardless of whether it is written or spoken. The image is something secondary and ancillary that has an explicative or propagandistic value.

The irony of fate has dictated that the vision of Brigitte Cornand in the documentary *Guy Debord, son art et son temps* (1994) arrives at the opposite conclusion. This documentary is put together with images from the television repertory (newscasts, cultural events), and contains some of most alarming and disturbing scenes of the last few years, with the filming of a little South American girl swallowed by a swamp following an earthquake, as well as the filming of an attempted lynching of a Somali woman accused by her fellow countrymen of having had sexual relations with soldiers of the UN troops sent to Africa. In these two sequences, the documentary aspect of the movie finds it highest excitement. Highly tragic events are captured on camera at the moment they occur without the operator introducing his own personal comment or judgement. On the contrary, live sound forces us to listen to the agonizing farewell of the little girl to her mother, and the riotous outcries that accompany the stripping of the Somali woman. These images raise theoretical problems in the most direct and effective way. Why is modern technology, which makes possible the shooting of similar tragedies the moment they occur, incapable of bringing practical help to the victims?

The case of the Somali woman is even more complex. In fact, the film shows that she is forced out of a UN military jeep by an angry crowd. In short, it seems as if the soldiers believe that the issue does not concern them, as if it were an issue that the Somalis have to work out among themselves. Their behaviour brings to mind Pontius Pilate, with the aggravation that they themselves are the cause of the lynching. To be sure, the soldiers are in Somalia on a peace mission, to resolve problems that the Somalis cannot solve for themselves. But between public and private facts, between military and sexual facts there is a big difference! By defending the woman they run a great risk to themselves, and, after all, the woman went to them of her own free choice knowing full well what the consequences would be! The filmed sequence also shows many other things. First of all the woman's attempt to get back on the jeep, and being rejected by one of the soldiers; the face and actions of her tormentors, for example, the young man who tries to hit her with a rock thrown by a slingshot, or the man who pursues her and gives her no respite, a true master of ceremony of the act of stoning, or so many others who beat her with clubs. Highly dramatic is the run of the woman who tries to find help from a passing car but is rejected by the passengers. Seized and brutally stripped, we see the pulling of the elastic of her bra amongst a vortex of fists, slaps, kicks. Then with a jump the woman succeeds in getting closer to a cart full of watermelons (did you ever think that in a lynching scene there could be watermelon slices?) and in grabbing a knife to defend herself. At the same time, someone pulls the lower part of her dress. The attempt to cover herself makes it impossible to focus on the weapon she has finally in her hand. Meanwhile someone grabs her by the wrist of the hand that wields the shining knife. At this point we are blinded by the beauty of the girl who completely naked seems to shine just as much as the blade of her weapon. In about ten frames an epiphany occurs that raises the poor girl to the Empyrean of the greatest images of eroticism in art and literature, beside the Judiths, Lucretias and Penthesileas. In the general confusion, she slips under the watermelon cart. The last image of the sequence shows a confused struggle of hands grabbing the knife.

Everything lasts fifty seconds but long enough to make the sensitive and educated spectator uncomfortable. To be sure, he thinks that what happened is terrible. But at issue here is not only the religious aspect, relative to the punishment of an adulteress, but even more important, the political one of collaborating with the enemy. The UN troops are perceived, no doubt, as enemies by the Islamic fundamentalists who claim, rightly or wrongly (on this the enlightened spectator does not pass judgement), that their survival depends on their capacity of being completely impermeable to the lifestyle of the West. Therefore, they must prevent by any means their women, who are attracted by the mirages of the West, from helping the enemy. To be sure, killing is a bit much, but stripping the women who slept with the enemy and carrying them naked through the streets is something that even the Resistance has done. (There is photographic documentation concerning the French, from which one can deduce the existence of a 'master of ceremonies' similar to the Somali.)[50] At that time, these women were called, with some irony, 'horizontal collaborators' and in all probability this treatment was considered more gallant and magnanimous than the one reserved for a male traitor.

The event fits within the logic of the war that prescribes capital punishment for traitors. However, the fact that it was filmed makes it intolerable for some. Why? There are two reasons that explain the discomfort, a cognitive and an ethical one. Both concern the empathic identification of the spectator with similar scenes. The first concerns the intellectual and cognitive aspect, the other the sensitive and emotional one. No doubt that they favour a naive acritical attitude with respect to video and cinema, almost as if they were mirrors of reality. In this sequence I can't see elements that put into question the authenticity of the facts depicted. However, the image of the soldier who looks on the scene more or less indifferently may have been added during the montage. Certainly, the more realistic, spontaneous and unforeseeable is the filming of the events, the more it wants to be believed absolutely. The image seems to provide an irrefutable proof that cancels any critical attitude, and exalts the 'issues of fact' with respect to 'issues of law.' Under this aspect, this type of film does not seem to favour the rise of a philosophical spirit. The second reason concerns the excitement generated in the spectator that resembles that of spectators at an execution, with the aggravation of absolute irresponsibility. The spectator finds himself in a situation that is morally more ambiguous than that of the actual culprits.

Therefore, the problem concerns the use to be made of a similar sequence. Should we place it in a 'library of images not seen' and invisible, of which Wenders speaks? Contrary to this view are the authors of the television show *Blob* who showed the scene and followed it with a striptease by an actress of erotic films. Its intellectual problematic and its emotional tonality are thus completely annulled, according to a premise similar to Debord's who considers that all images are interchangeable. To others, however, the images of the attempted lynching of the Somali woman did not seem similar to a striptease,[51] and not to me either. Not for naive reasons of 'subject matter' but for strictly cinematographic reasons. In those fifty seconds, in fact, the operator fully realizes an intention pursued by the cinema ever since its origins, documenting a unique event in the moment in which it occurs and becoming, insofar as film fact goes, a unique event.

4. Iconoclastic Undinism

If for Wenders the images are 'for sale' and for Debord they are interchangeable, there is someone who has succeeded in making a film entirely without images, that stands entirely on sound, namely Derek Jarman in his last film *Blue* (1993). And yet it is not a radio play but a film. For the entire duration of the film, the colour blue is projected continuously, while the sound is a kind of poetic diary with musical accompaniment in which Jarman, terminally ill with Aids, registers his progressive loss of sight and the dramatic deterioration of his health. It is a documentary film, par excellence, based on the identity between life and cinema, illness and art, rich in passages sometimes ironic, sometimes heart-rending, which asks, however, to be considered a work of art and not simply the protocol of an agony. In the last few years, the field of visual anthropology has seen the spreading of a tendency that considers filming to be so much more scientifically interesting the lesser is the author's intervention.[52] We run the risk, in this fashion, of falling into a naive attitude which, in uniting scientism with spontaneity, imagines that the truth can be offered entirely naked to the video recorder or to the camera without any mediation. Jarman's film, precisely for its dramatically autobiographical character, shows instead that even the most personal and most subjective confession is always, in film (as in a book), a *staged authenticity*, a truth-effect. But this is not a limitation of the work. On the contrary, it's its greatness. What matters is not the dying documented in its immediacy, but what Jarman makes of his dying. Let us suppose that he did not die at all later, in fact, that he was not even sick and that the entire film was a product of his imagination, not a documentary but a fiction. Would something change? I would say yes. In fact, we would see that what Jarman imagines is what an Aids patient feels, not what Jarman has done with his illness. In short, with *Blue* we are in a zone which is different both from fiction and from protocol, and which is decentralized with respect to both the imagination and lived life, even if it is in relation to both.

Blue is as unitarian a film as possible. It satisfies fully the philosophical attitude to lead the great variety of the world back to a very few entities. In this case, the title sums up the literal aspects of experience as well as the metaphoric ones, namely, the darkening and progressive loss of sight, which is not only told but also proposed and imposed on the spectator; the colour of the sea, which occupies a central place in Jarman's imaginary; the state of depression and sadness in which he sinks, in accordance to the figurative meaning from which the word American *blues* comes from; finally the horizon of transgressive sexual experiences from which his illness derives and to which one remains loyal because it constitutes a destiny (*blue movie* is a pornographic movie). The dimensions of the 'blue experience' are four: abolition of images, the oceanic sentiment of life, beyond the pleasure principle, and perverse sexuality. A long tradition has accustomed us to establishing a close relation between aniconicity and religious patriarchal monotheism. The absolute transcendence of God goes along with the prohibition of making sacred images. Jarman's aniconicity, instead, has completely different theoretical and emotional bases. It is the result of a loss of identity and individual form into an indistinct entity, into the primordial ocean, into the great Uroboric mother,[53] into a feminine archetype imagined as anterior and posterior with respect to our individual existence. The great psychologist of sexuality Henry Havelock Ellis has defined with the term 'undinism' the attraction for water together with urethral eroticism.[54] In fact, Jarman seems to be very close to the origins where Ellis has derived its name, the romantic tale of *Undine* by Friedrich de la Motte-Fouqué. Here, as in *Blue*, sexuality, the call of water and death are united in the unerasable memory of past love.

5. Deafness and Estrangement

If we took away the words, instead of the images, we would return to the early phase of cinema history, to the silent movie. It would be a merely regressive process. The film by Nicholas Philibert, *Le pays des sourds*, (1992), moves instead toward the discovery of new horizons. It is a documentary on the conditions of the deaf from birth who express themselves through sign language, a code that takes the place of phonic language. The essence of the film, however, is not, in my view, in the contrast between sound and deaf culture. This comparison could very well be resolved in favour of the latter, as an extremely eloquent professor of sign language suggests through his hand gestures: 'My wife and I are both non hearing and, to be sure, we would have preferred a deaf kid, but our daughter hears pretty well, but we love her just the same!' It is not a question so much of turning a disability into a gift, a defect into a quality, as a question of venturing along a path which is accessible only through the experience of a handicap. Philibert does not propose a regression toward a world of silence, but the access to an horizon in which silence and words strengthen one another.

Diderot in his *Letter on the Deaf and Dumb* (1749) tells us that the writer Le Sage, who had become deaf in his old age, would go anyway to the performance of his plays. 'He said he was a better judge of his plays and their action when he could no longer hear the actors.'[55] In short, it would seem as if the deprivation of hearing is compensated by the acquisition of a 'look from outside', an external point of view extraneous to needs and desires, which is essentially philosophical. Not by chance, Siegfried Kracauer situated the essence of cinema in this estrangement, almost as if it marked the access to an alternative experience to daily life.[56] Maybe the cinema is capable of giving us what common philosophical writing can only grant with difficulty, namely, an impersonal and suspended feeling, or, as Wittgenstein said: 'a coloured and intense *epoché*.'[57]

5
The Third System of Art

1. Art without Aura, Criticism without Theory

In the youthful world of art criticism the opinion that today's art can do without theory is common. Thus, the task of the art critic should be limited to a kind of report and promotional work for the artists that he likes, without getting involved in questions of poetics and history of art, let alone aesthetics. This view is a comprehensible reaction to the tenuousness and inconclusive wordiness of so much art criticism of the second half of the twentieth century, with which the young generation is in harsh polemic. But the view is also based on deeper intuitions that have their roots in the artistic trends of the 1990s which, as the *Post human* shows, seem characterized by a total flattening of the existent, by an ultra-naturalism alien from any transcendence even if just theoretical, by a sensibility permeated by disgust and abjection. It would seem, therefore, that the youthful world of art criticism, instead of explaining the artists of the *Post human* to the public, may want to enter into competitive relation with them, adopting from their message not the extremism of their provocations and transgressions, but the monotony, the banality and 'idiocy' of their works. After all, on this anti-theoretical orientation, art criticism lines up ultimately with youthful music, cinema and literary criticism. The most paradoxical aspect of this orientation is that the flattening of the existent does not exempt them at all from expressing a judgement on the artists. In fact, this type of criticism is full of evaluations, opinions, and rejections entirely groundless and superficial. To look closer, this does not depend at all on the fact that the critic vindicates for himself the freedom of the artist, but on the attitude of the amateur who expresses a judgement of personal and private taste, which does not go beyond: 'I like this', 'I don't like that.'

2. On the Credibility of Art and the Uniqueness of the Artist

Walter Benjamin's essay, 'The Work of Art in the Age of Mechanical Reproduction',[58] constitutes a reference point of great importance on the question of the importance of theory for the plastic arts today. As we know, Benjamin's essay stands on the contrast between the traditional system of the work of art, characterized by the *aura*, that is, by the cultural value attributed to a unique and lasting object, which favours an aesthetic experience based on a relation of distance with respect to the user, and the fully secularized and disenchanted system opened up by the mechanical reproduction of the work of art, which confers on it a merely expository value and initiates a relation of proximity with the public. Benjamin does not discuss the problem of the role of theoretical mediation in the constitution of artistic value in the two systems. However, it would be wrong to deduce from the standardization inherent in the second system that it no longer has any need of theory. Benjamin is without doubt extraneous to any type of populist outcome, which to him is closer to Fascism that 'sees its salvation in giving these masses a chance to express themselves'.[59] In the era of mechanical reproduction, the fundamental task of theory seems to be, rather, that of considering art from a secular and disenchanted point of view. Therefore, on the one hand, theory cannot go back toward the *aura*, on the other, neither can it abolish itself and let the public establish empirically and immediately what is and what is not art.

If we consider the event of the plastic arts from the 1960s on, it seems that it follows a path very different from the one outlined by Benjamin. In fact, he relates the disappearance of the *aura* with the dissolution of the criterion of authenticity of the work of art and with the transformation of the author into some kind of technical operator. Now these three elements of art – *aura*, work, and author – have undergone unexpected transformations. As far as the permanence of a transcendental dimension, not unlike a religious one, in the experience of art is concerned, one can question that the secularization has actually taken place. The religious paradigm articulated on the three figures of the prophet, the faithful, and the priest has been considered relevant for explaining the artistic paradigm articulated on the respective figures of artist, public and specialist.[60] Furthermore, it has seemed necessary to the very survival of the artistic object an attitude of 'belief' that would allow it to assert its difference with respect to the objects of daily life.[61] As for the principle of authenticity of the work of art, there is no question that it has been extraordinarily reinforced. In fact, the more the artistic object is indistinguishable from the utilitarian object, as

in the *ready made,* the more it has to be certified and guaranteed as
unique, unrepeatable and endowed with cultural authority. In fact,
the artist is involved in a process of unprecedented singularization
which has even broken those principles of universality on which the
experience of eighteenth-century aesthetics onward was founded.
Singularity and its more transgressive manifestations have finally
become the only criterion of the value of today's art.

3. Beyond the Aura and Mechanical Reproduction

We are not doing justice to Benjamin's essay if we limit ourselves to
considering the opposition between the regime of *aura* and that of
mechanical reproduction. We ignore its most important theoretical
contribution, namely, the one connected to the determination of
a third regime of art and aesthetic experience, characterized by reification, fetishism, and more generally, by that phenomenon that he
himself defined as 'the *sex appeal* of the inorganic'. Within the
perspective of this third dimension, irreducible and different from
the other two, we can finally comprehend the dynamics of contemporary art, which is neither religious in the traditional sense, nor
mechanical in the functional sense of the term, but partakes of the
pathology of religious experience in the form of fetishism, as well as
of technological imagination in the form of animation of the not
living. Benjamin refers to this third dimension when he emphasizes
the confusion between actor and tool, human being and thing,
inherent in the shooting of a film, or when he sees in the performance of a movie actor a reification not only of his work force, but
also of his body, skin, hair, heart, and kidneys. It is precisely in
contemporary art that this mixture of materiality and abstraction
finds its most extreme manifestation. In fact, in it, the personality of
the artist is transformed in a brand name that guarantees the value
of artistic merchandise. The formal characteristics of the latter lose
importance and can even be substituted by an idea, as is the case, in
fact, in conceptual art.

A truly singular aspect of contemporary art consists in the fact
that however radical its demystification has been, that is, the baring
of economical and institutional devices that support it, it has com-
promised very little of its cultural credibility and none at all of its
commercial and worldly credibility. The fact is that what has
deprived art of its *aura* has not only been the revolutionary thought

from Benjamin to Debord, from Castoriadis to Baudrillard, but what has also contributed to this unveiling, in much greater measure, are the artists themselves from Duchamp to Warhol, from Fontana to Boltanski, from Christo to Beyus, authors whose works are no less radical than the thinkers.

4. Modern and Contemporary Paradigms

As it was shown recently by a sociologist of French art, Nathalie Heinich, in *Le triple jeu de l'art contemporain*,[62] the entire vicissitudes of contemporary art can be interpreted as a transgression of frontiers and as an extraordinary widening of its territory. However, such crossing of limits must not be understood as an absence of norms but as a complex strategy of challenges and scandals, which seem to fall more within communication and information than within those artistic products understood as objects to be collected. Incidentally, Heinich's distinction between modern and contemporary paradigms seems relevant here. For the modern paradigm, the artistic value resides in the work and all that is external to it is added to the intrinsic value of the work. Whereas in the contemporary paradigm, the artistic value resides in the combination of connections (discourses, actions, grids, situations and sense effects) established around or starting from an object, which is only an occasion, a pretext, or a point of transition.

Now, there is no doubt that the modern paradigm corresponds perfectly to what in the Introduction I indicated as 'the art of works of art'; somewhat more uncertain is the identification of the contemporary paradigm with media vitalism. By 'contemporary paradigm', Nathalie Heinich understands, rather, an intermediary situation between the art of works of art and artistic communication, in which public artistic institution (namely big museums and international exhibitions) play a primary role in both fields, that of the valorization of works of art and of media events. In fact, unlike the past, there is agreement between the institution and the transgressive media artist at the expense of the third term of the 'game of contemporary art', the public. That is to say, while in the past the institution shared the point of view of the public and condemned the transgressive operations of the avant-garde, today instead the institution believes it to be more convenient to support and favour the transgressive artist, because it gains a much greater benefit from the scandal in terms of publicity and media exposure than what it could obtain from adhering to traditional public taste. Thus, an avant-garde art is born which is directly in touch with the institutions, which has succeeded in reaching, at times, market quotations higher than those that rely on private galleries and collections. The privileged customer of the new transgressive artist is no longer the merchant, nor the farsighted collector (as in the modern paradigm), but the institution itself! The break between artistic innovation and the public has increased enormously, to the point of becoming a really insoluble conflict. The public can be compared to the spectator of a chess game who does not know the rules of the game. He sees two people taking turns in moving some statuettes on a checkered board. At the same time, however, the acceptance on the part of institutions annuls the transgressive effect of artistic innovation and transforms the entire system of art into a game for beginners from which, as Nathalie Heinich correctly points out, are absent those who could still get angry!

How to avoid this situation that ends up by generating a profound malaise not only in the public but also in most artists and mediators (critics, curators, and theorists of art)? In the first place, we need to abandon the idea that transgression in itself constitutes an effective type of opposition. If the movement that characterized modern art, from the second half of the nineteenth century to today, was transgression, it has completely exhausted its polemical function. An opposition determined on the basis of what it denies already appeared to Nietzsche as a merely reactionary attitude, incapable of asserting the autonomy of its own difference. Already in *The Wanderer and His Shadow* he defined it as 'the sickness from one's chains'. Today's art still suffers from this sickness and it has not yet shown to be completely healthy. These chains are 'those heavy and pregnant errors contained in the conceptions of morality, religion and metaphysics.' [350].[63] It is not enough to demystify art by depriving it of its *aura*, which constitutes precisely the metaphysical, moral and religious way in which the difference of the work of art has been thought with respect to the world. This demystification, which Benjamin linked to the advent of mechanical reproduction, ends up by levelling art at the most insignificant reality, reducing it to an instrument of recreation and edifying spectacle. Very eloquently, Gianni Vattimo has emphasized the importance of completing the process of demystification through an 'unmasking of the unmasking'.[64] In fact, demystification reveals itself to be functional with respect to the demands of a society that no longer has any need to maintain the relative autonomy of symbolical activities such as art, philosophy and, more generally, humanistic studies. Therefore, it tends to transform the bearers of symbolic activities in 'functionaries of the productive system, levelling them to a relation of immediate reference to the exigencies of production and social organization'.[65] Under this aspect, *Posthuman* art without *aura* and criticism without theory that promotes it would constitute a considerable acceleration of this process. The transgression of the frontiers of art would not be at all a progressive movement, but would aim at taking away any autonomy from the artist, the critic, and the curator, bringing them back to the level of reality, that is, of direct dependence on economical imperatives. Under this aspect, the vindication of the *aura* of works of art and the autonomy of symbolical worlds would take on today the meaning of social contestation because it would constitute the last defence with respect to the total and direct dominion of capital. Instead, paradoxically, whoever works against cultural mediation, in favour of communicative and expositive spontaneity, notwithstanding its progressive intentions, would only accomplish the acceleration of the process of liquidation of symbolical worlds.

The fact is that the 'contemporary paradigm' described by Heinich, to which adhere the majority of the largest institutions of art today, does not follow at all the road of demystification and unmasking, but promotes a hyper-mystification. On the one hand, it exaggerates the singularity of the artist, on the other, it dissolves all contents of his/her personality. On the one hand, it still proposes works of art to the appreciation of the public, on the other, it proceeds according to unprincipled strategies of self-promotion that have nothing more to do with art. In other words, the artist, the critic, and the theorist of art find themselves having to reckon with very shady situations in which the mixture of cynicism, commercial interests and personal rivalry hinder a correct professional practice. Compared to these situations, both the traditional defence of the *aura*, as well as the path of unmasking and extreme transgression turn out to be losers. In fact, the 'contemporary paradigm' does not deny the *aura*, but mystifies it through the hyperbolic economic evaluation of the signature of some artists promoted by strategies that belong to the communication market and not to that of art.

It does not even deny transgression, but renders it inoperative, because it appropriates it to its own advantage.

5. *The Heroic–Ironic Role of Art and Philosophy*

All this notwithstanding, the 'contemporary paradigm' of art must be viewed as one of the most exciting aspects of contemporary culture, precisely because of this incongruous mixture of economic, aesthetic and communicative aspects. To reflect on this phenomenon is good not only for sociology, as Nathalie Heinich claims in her brilliant pamphlet, *Ce que l'art fait à la sociologie*,[66] but, perhaps, even more for philosophy. In fact, while for sociology, art is (at least according to Heinich) only an object of study that obliges it to refine its own instruments of inquiry, for philosophy it is something even closer, because it also partakes of that regimen of singularity, which is constructed on oneness, irreducibility, originality and transgression of canons, on which the world of art stands. For instance, it becomes difficult to consider 'good' a philosophical work just because it reaches a certain standard. In fact, to assign it this qualification, it means to discredit it, that is, to consider it devoid of those requisites of innovation and creativity that are thought to be essential to philosophical production. Thus, the expression 'philosophical career' sounds just as reductive as 'artistic career' because it implies the standardization of what by definition is modelled on the imperative of exceptionality. As Heinich keenly remarks, the exercise of art is precisely the opposite of a bureaucratic career. While the latter pursues personal goals (i.e. self-promotion) through impersonal methods (the application of rules), the artist and the philosopher pursue impersonal goals (the opening of horizons of experience characterized by a claim to universality) by personal means (the protection and development of one's own singularity).

What can no longer be proposed is the idea of an artist or an organic thinker, that is, a producer of innovations, who derives his own credibility uniquely on the fact of expressing the ideas and mode of feeling of a community. In fact, this idea, in turn, presupposes that today a community exists, based on nation, religion, class, sex or some other data, that possesses a unique identity. It is interesting to observe that also within so-called *Cultural Studies*, the same notions of culture and value come into collision with one another. The concept of culture (or subculture) seems, in fact, tied to a normative presupposition of the traditionalist and conservative type, which in the last instance, appeals to principles of purity, integrity, and social vitality. In the sphere of art and philosophy, the valorization would imply, instead, the promotion of choices and transgressive strategies with respect to canons that can be understood only by those who have the knowledge and instruments to understand them and that, therefore, would tend to be constituted as an autonomous social group possessing specific interests.[68]

On the other hand, the productions of art and philosophy have always solicited for themselves a universal recognition, however potential and virtual. Therefore, the innovation with respect to previous models can never be too great, lest one falls back into extravagance and inaccessibility. Thus, the artist and the philosopher tend to recognize themselves in an 'heroic–ironic' role[69] which, on the one hand, contains an element of defiance with respect to what is socially dominant, but, on the other, cannot get exhausted in transgression, lest one persists in that state of subordination with respect to the past that Nietzsche defined as the 'sickness from one's chains'.

The question which is not easy to answer is whether this 'heroic–ironic' role is more consonant today with the philosopher or the artist. The latter, in fact, seems to be too entangled in the ambiguities and in the inconsistencies of the 'contemporary paradigm' to be able to reach that *third system of art and aesthetic experience* that lies beyond the traditional *aura* and mechanical disenchantment. Paradoxically, therefore, the philosopher of art seems today to be better equipped than the artist to valorize, without remaining prisoner of the cult of works of art, and to communicate, without being victimized by the realistic coarseness of an immediate transmission.

6. Greatness, Justification, Compromise

What is certain is that both art and philosophy need to be *put to the test,* that is, to be confronted with certain external situations, to the microartistic milieu and the philosophical institution, respectively. From this test depends the possibility to gain access to new forms of greatness that would heal them from the 'sickness from one's chains', namely, from restorations and transgressions. What characterizes this putting to the test is the confrontation with things, as Luc Boltanski and Laurent Thévenot remark in *De la justification.*[70] *Les économies de la grandeur.* The value of people, objects and actions are strictly connected among themselves, and it is precisely from the discovery of this mutual relation that the *third system of art* originates where the appreciation is not centred solely on singularity, on the work, or on communication.

This requires a comprehensive reflection of the notion of *greatness* to which Boltanski and Thévenot make a very important contribution. In the first place, one should leave behind the metaphysical idea of greatness, which is based solely on the intrinsic property of a person, an object or an action. The theory of *aura* falls, precisely, within this first conception of greatness which departs from the existence of common worlds. On the contrary, the notion of greatness must be thought of with reference to the plurality of political contexts that are determined in historical experience. Therefore, an absolute greatness does not exist, only various *political systems of greatness*. Boltanski and Thévenot single out six that correspond to as many worlds, and they examine their characteristics in detail through an examination of the authors who have theorized about them in the first place, namely, the inspired city (Augustine), the domestic city (Bossuet), the city of opinions (Hobbes), the civic city (Rousseau), the commercial city (Smith), and the industrial city (Saint-Simon).

The anchoring of the notion of greatness to specific worlds and concrete situations makes it possible to avoid the opposite danger to metaphysics, that is, the nihilistic relativism that behind every greatness there is misery and behind every misery a will to power. This perspective, even though it refers all too often to the notion of 'interest', nonetheless, does not belong to the economic sphere which entails the sacrifice of the individual's drives, in consideration of a general idea of greatness. According to Boltanski and Thévenot, secularization and disenchantment self-destruct when pushed to an extreme. They rupture any political tie and make one regress toward the search for 'a self-satisfaction that no longer is preoccupied with establishing an agreement with others',[71] that is, toward an infantilism that they define as the 'rejoicing in the happiness of being young'.[72] Nihilism, therefore, would be a form of infantilism for, in fact, kids do not yet have access to any type of generality, that is, to 'a universe subjected to the obligation of justification' in which 'the rationality of behaviour can be put to the test'.[73]

It is important that Boltanski and Thévenot recognize to the world of inspiration (within which the practice of art and philosophy

is included) a *political* meaning that cannot be subordinated at all
to other worlds. In other words, the practice of art and philosophy
are not private matters: 'In a world in which human beings are
appreciated for their *oneness* and in which the most general is the
most *original*, the greats are both unique and universal.'[74] Heinich
has developed this aspect much further. According to her, so far, the
social sciences have not recognized the importance of singularity
and uniqueness as factors of production and action. They have
adopted reductive criteria taking for granted the superiority of the
social with respect to the singular. The reduction to the social is not
a judgment of fact, but of value. It is absurd that disciplines, such as
sociology, which pretend to be descriptive and non normative, remain victim of these prejudices. It is not at all a question of the
re-evaluating the ontological meaning of singularity but of 'settling
in the observation of the construction of values', by taking seri-
ously the motivations provided by the actors.[75] Instead of imposing
in an authoritative and dogmatic way the primacy of the social, it
is necessary 'to place in evidence the plurality of systems of action
and axiological systems'[76] passing from the analysis of essences to
that of representations. In other words, it is not important to know
whether originality exists or is an illusion, but to know through
which operation it is constructed, maintained and dissolved.

The conception of society as something organic and unitarian
is a sociological myth. The various worlds singled out by Boltanski
and Thévenot are profoundly different from each other. The task
of the theorist is not to propose models of total harmonization and
synthesis. These models, in whose invention the aesthetic has precisely exercised its phantasy, conceal the concrete situations in which
human beings interact. However, we must not associate either, in-
dissolubly, a specific group with every world. 'Every person faces
daily situations that depend on distinct worlds, which he must be
able to recognize, and prove capable of adapting to them.'[77] But
this adaptation can occur in two ways, through an *arrangement* or
through a *compromise*, but only in the latter case is the search for
a common good kept in mind. The *arrangement*, instead, is a contingent agreement related to the convenience of the two parts, without
legitimacy and non-universalizable. The reciprocal concessions on
which an *arrangement* is based aim at stopping the dissensus without going back to the motivations on which the different assess-
ments of the greatness of people, things or actions at play stand.

Only in *compromise* does the search for an agreement lead the contenders to raise themselves above contingencies and formulate a *justification* for one's own words, behaviour and actions. Without *justification*, therefore, neither greatness nor agreement is possible.

If in the light of this ambitious sociological theory one reflects on the case of the 'contemporary paradigm' of art, we realize right away that it stands, more or less, on *arrangements* and not on *compromises*. Instances from the world of inspiration, the world of commerce, and the world of opinion converge in arrangements whose supporting principles are, in most cases, not self-evident. All this not only generates disorientation in the public but also in many artists, critics and insiders, and ends up by placing art outside of any possible greatness. However, the sociological works to which we have referred reduce the possibility of mystification and bragging. In fact, they place the problem of the so-called 'artistic values' in a concrete way and watchful of specific situations. The trend in which they find themselves tends to study closely the dynamics of valorization and devaluation, thus overcoming the limitations of an approach whose values are too abstract (typical of the philosophy of art) or too superficial and extrinsic (typical of the sociology of art). It also entails a profound theoretical renewal which reveals itself in a meaningful conceptual innovation with respect to traditional aesthetics. The place of judgement is taken by justification, that of genius by competence, that of taste by the admiration for greatness. In the third system of art other artificial oppositions also tend to fail. These are the conditions whereby artists and critics, curators and theorists, find themselves united in a single struggle.

6
Art and Remainder

1. *Philosophy and the Other Arts*

A new German collection of philosophical books carries a title that deserves attention, *Philosophie und andere Künste*. It synthesizes extremely well an emerging tendency in the world of philosophy, and particularly in aesthetics, which consists of considering philosophical activity closer to the arts than to the sciences. Now, the idea that a philosophical text can be the object of a reading similar to that of a literary text is nothing new. Hermeneutics, post-structuralism and deconstruction have pursued and explored this path, expanding and renewing in a decisive manner the methods of historiographical research and textual inquiry. However, in these contexts, the similarity remains limited to the encounter between philosophy and literature, singling out within these literary genres that of philosophical literature.

The stakes are different in the expression 'Philosophy and the other arts'. Here it is not simply a question of considering the textual aspect of philosophy, but of understanding philosophy as an art *sui generis* possessing specific characteristics and yet reducible under the common heading of art. And here the difficulties begin, since, even though it should not be too difficult to grasp the specific difference of philosophy with respect to the other arts, it becomes quite problematic, instead, to determine what is art today.

My aim in this chapter consists first of all of exploring two artistic trends that have moved in the direction of philosophy, expanding considerably the limits of the traditional notion of art and confronting aesthetic theory with new problems difficult to resolve. The two movements that I intend to take into account are the Situationist's anti-art and Kosuth's conceptual art.

2. *Situationist's Anti-Art and the Event*

Within the context of the numerous artistic movements that in the course of the twentieth century contested the very notion of art, the Situationist International was the most radical and one that led to an actual rejection of art. And yet the movement, originating in Italy in 1957, appeared in its first phase still under the aspect of an artistic avant-garde. But soon its modernist tendencies were condemned and any artistic practice was drastically stigmatized as 'anti-situationist'.[78] In fact, the theoretical wing prevails, in the person of Guy Debord, who focuses the attention of the Situationist International on the critique of neo-capitalist society. It is worth asking about the meaning of this turn which marks the estrangement from the movement of important artists such as Asger Jorn, Pinot-Gallizio and the architect Constant. Reflecting on the subsequent development of the movement, which finds its apogee in the 1960s and later dissolves in the following couple of years amongst polemics and expulsions, one could be tempted to think that Debord had led the Situationist International to a nullity, uprooting very promising artistic and creative potentialities, and shutting himself and his companions in the blind alley of political extremism. In other words, that Debord was incapable of providing his movement with that amplitude and richness of perspective and development that André Breton was able to secure for Surrealism; that the Situationist International took from Surrealism its worst aspects, that is, the sectarianism and the practice of defamatory expulsions, without, however, inheriting its dynamic and force of attraction; that the cause of this failure ought to be looked for in an anti-aesthetic and iconoclastic moralism, whose origins go back to the Reformation. Under this aspect, Debord's critique of contemporary society of the spectacle would be the contemporary equivalent of the millenary rejection of art and the Calvinist condemnation of theatre. In Debord, only the anti-aesthetic and anti-worldly orientation of the sixteenth century's religious revolution would remain alive and working.

Now, I do not deny that this religious heritage was present in the International, but I would like to claim that the anti-artistic choice of Debord has an aesthetic meaning and that precisely from this aspect derives the present interest in his thinking. At first sight it may seem that for Debord the *after* of art is the critical theory of society. Radical philosophy would be the heir of the artistic avant-garde, which tends, precisely, to disappear and to dissolve in revolutionary theory. However, in Debord any propensity towards utopia is missing. His attention has always been focused on the present conflict instead of future harmony. From this derives, precisely, that 'toughness' that accompanied him throughout his life and made it possible, as he says, 'to be in war with the entire world, with a light heart'.[79]

This 'toughness', in my view, has a stoic-cynical colouring that constitutes the key for comprehending the notion from which the Situationist International takes its name, that is, from the situation. It assumes its full meaning in opposition to the spectacle. While the spectacle is a 'social relation among individuals, mediated by images',[80] the situation is, rather, an event, a dimension of the happening which implies a strong experience of the present and entails a certain coincidence of freedom and destiny. Neither Debord nor any other Situationist has defined the situation this way. What I am proposing, therefore, is an a posteriori definition of the idea of situation that moreover exclusively concerns Debord. In fact, the sense given by most Situationists to this notion is vitiated by a subjective and vitalistic accentuation that belongs to the culture of the period and that represents the most short-lived aspect of the movement. Therefore, Giorgio Agamben is correct when, presenting the work of Debord to the Italian public in 1990, he establishes a link between the notion of situation and Nietzsche's idea of the 'eternal return of the same'.[81] The situation is not at all the creative spontaneity that shrinks from any objectivation, it is not the gushing vitality that does not let itself be captured in any form, it is not even the liberation of subjectivity.

To begin from the moment in which one understands the situation as event, one understands that Debord's anti-artistic choice is not necessarily an anti-aesthetic choice, also. The abandonment of art does not also imply automatically the abandonment of the aesthetic horizon. In fact, ever since ancient Greece, aesthetic feeling has come to be determined on the basis of an opposition between two opposite modes of conceiving beauty. On the one hand it was thought of as form, according to a perspective oriented toward the appreciation of works of art, on the other it was thought of as event, according to a perspective oriented toward the experience of surprise, electrocution, something irreducible to the quiet contemplation of rational essences. It was the classical Italian philologist Carlo Diano who proposed an interpretation of the Greek world based, precisely, on the opposition between the two principles of form and event [1952].[82] He made a very important contribution to the determination of what an event is: 'It is not enough that something happens to call it an event. In order for it to be an event it is necessary that I feel that this is a happening for me.'[83] Therefore, not every happening is an event, but only the one that presents itself as *tyche*. What did the Greeks mean by this word? Originally, it was perceived as the opposite of *amartía*, which means shooting a bullet that does not hit the target and, therefore, a mistake, an error, sin, fault.[84] Therefore, in the word *tyche* is inherent the idea of success. This is in perfect conformity to the sensibility of the Situationist which is always characterized not only by a very strong sense of its own excellence but also by a profound faith in its own historical success. The origin of this attitude, which manifested itself under the aspect of a real triumph, must be sought not so much in the Hegelian-Marxism professed by the Situationist International, as in the stoic-cynical attitude of Guy Debord and his aesthetics of the 'grand style'.[85]

Anyhow, it is only by closely examining the research on *tyche* that we can clarify the theoretical problems relative to the notion of situation. In Pindar, who calls it *tycha*, it is 'the expression of a situation of "grace" that interprets the experience of victory'.[86] In the writers of the classical period, its meaning shifts between chance (which the Greeks called *autómaton*) and fortune (a word that belongs to Latin culture). Defined as 'a cause not apparent to human reasoning', the notion of *tyche* plays a great role in the work of the historian Thucydides. In his view, *tyche* is 'why reality differs from reasoning, but also what the best reasoning must adapt to'.[87] To *tyche* belong those events of which one cannot give a rational explanation, namely the fact that a human being has determined physical characteristics, that he is born in a certain environment, that certain events happen to him, etc. The word *tyche*, rather than designating the word 'chance' (*caso*), which contains certain philosophical implications, is closer to the 'events' of life, and can be more conveniently translated as 'destiny' (*sorte*).

The most profound meditation on this theme was done by the Stoics, for whom destiny coincided with liberty, factuality with rationality, the external aspect of what occurs suddenly and without a logical cause and the internal aspect of what appears to conform to the subjectivity and the rationality of the single. As Aldo Magris points out, Stoicism is irreducible to Socratic subjectivism which only differentiates between what-is-in-us from what does not depend on us, and which, therefore, remains imprisoned in a narrow conception of the wise man. To consider self-awareness a guarantee of freedom means forgetting that what I am and what I think belong objectively to the world. For the Stoics, necessity and liberty are both part of destiny. They ask the individual to become part of a design greater than his conscience, and to give it his approval and, thus, to direct his subjective will in the direction required by an external rationality. In other words, there is an event when, instead of remaining prisoners of an internal/external opposition, between subjectivity and world, I find a constructive solution that would allow me to posit myself positively within a process that goes beyond myself.

This manner of conceiving the event leads to the assertion of an entirely original aesthetic dimension, new with respect to previous philosophies characterized 'by a kind of *"engagement dégagé"* '[88] which confers on action a decisive importance, separating it from practical results. For this reason, in the ancient world, Stoic behaviour was compared not to the medical or to the navigational arts, which at all costs had to reach their objectives, but to the dancer, who has within himself his own realization. There is no event without exercise, there is no situation without repetition. What is asserted as the best for me must be repeated, transformed, elaborated in what I want subjectively. Therefore, under a certain aspect the situation is a 'transit from the same to the same' through which a radical difference is fulfilled.[89] Only in this fashion can a work become an event, that is, something that happens for me, even though it is not my subjectivity to determine its concrete aspect.

From this aesthetic of the event originates the idea of art as exercise. As Gianni Carchia observed shrewdly, what counts in Stoic thinking is not the work of art but the exercise, that is, the process that leads to it, the productive movement that realizes it. This leads to a poetics of the grand style, to an extreme care of the expression, to the search for extreme refinement. It is not by chance that these are traits that we find in the writings of Guy Debord. Distance from the world, aesthetics of the struggle and live contact with history have constituted, in fact, the peculiar traits of his way of being, which have their roots in a stoic-cynical sensibility developed through a familiarity with the French writers of the seventeenth century.

3. Conceptual Art and the Non-Identity of Art

The second moment in which the paths of art and philosophy have come close to the point of being confused is represented by conceptual art. If with Debord and the Situationists, art seems to end in philosophy, with Kosuth and conceptual artists, philosophy seems to end in art. There is between the two movements a kind of parallelism even if they move in opposite directions. What brings them together is first of all the rejection of form. Kosuth is very polemical with respect to modernism, responsible in his view for the prevalence of a merely formal and organic conception of art. 'Formalist critics and artists alike,' writes Kosuth in his most important programmatic work of 1969, *Art after Philosophy and After*, 'do not question the nature of art [...] Being an artist now means to question the nature of art.'[90] Therefore, art does not consist in the production of forms and objects having a particular status, but in the broadening of the notion of art. Therefore, art is a post-philosophical activity for at least two reasons. In the first place because philosophers confine themselves to propose a static concept of art instead of widening its boundaries. In the second place because they seem to have abandoned even this function and to have reduced themselves to mere *librarians of truth*. The 'value' of particular artists after Duchamp can be weighed according to 'what they *added* to the conception of art' (K 18). The loss of credibility of art during the twentieth century was a consequence of modernism that transformed works of art into 'objects functioning as religious relics' (K 16), basing their value on economic bases only, that is, on the shortage of products endowed with *aura*. For Kosuth, the test of art is precisely the conquest of its credibility, as Gabriele Guercio who presented Kosuth's work in Italy remarks. The contemporary artist 'lives exposed to the risk that the truth borne from one's own experience is irremediably eclipsed by the presumed physicality of the works of art' (K 11).

Thus, a question emerges clearly that was latent in the Situationists, namely, the question of *residue*. If the essential of art is the activity of the artist, works of art are only a physical residue, the rest of something which is more important and essential. 'The collectors are irrelevant for the "artistic condition" of a work' (K 19), which is in a relation of opposition with the spectacle staged by *mass media*, and the entertainment they provide. A work of art is only the presentation of an artist's intention who tautologically certifies this quality. The conceptual artist, thus, annexes to himself the functions of the critic and turns to a public of artists. Therefore, just as with science, contemporary art does not allow a 'naive' approach.

It implies a preliminary knowledge of the 'state of art', of the situation in which it finds itself. In theory, nothing prevents the historians and the critics of art from also being considered artists. If this does not occur, it depends on the fact that they transform 'culture into nature' (K 68), that is, they remain prisoners of a morphological and organic conception of art. To place emphasis on the activity of the artist, therefore, does not entail justifying a naive subjectivism. Not everything is possible in art: in fact, conceptual art by posing as the heir of philosophy tends to present its own idea of art as an historical destiny.

The answer of the institutions to Kosuth's provoking ideas was not late in coming. In the 1970s George Dickie had already overturned Kosuth's premises. It is not the individual artist who decides what is art but the *art world*. Thus, Dickie formulates an *institutional theory of art* whereby a work of art is an artefact that presents its own candidacy for the appreciation of a few people who work on behalf of institutions.[91] Therefore, there is no such a thing as an essence of art, or a special aesthetic perception different from daily life. The theory elaborated by Dickie has two polemical objectives: aesthetic essentialism, on the one hand, which holds that it is possible to single out and define the identity of art, and, on the other, artistic conceptualism, which believes that this identity is not something static, or definable once and for all, but is broadened from time to time by the activity of the artists. Aesthetic essentialism seems to be too tied up by metaphysical premises. It peddles as universally valid criteria and tastes that are strictly dependent on socio-historical factors. Artistic conceptualism, for which the identity of art depends on the decision of the artist, appears to concede too much, instead, to subjective will. It reproposes the Romantic notion of genius, emancipating it from any limitation and emptying it of any content. Aesthetic institutionalism constitutes a kind of middle way between these two opposite theories. On the one hand, it considers art as an historical and not as a metaphysical category, on the other, it introduces elements of objectivity even too empirically definable. Therefore, it has been the target of much criticism, the most interesting of which, in my view, being the one that accuses the institutional theory of art of conforming and reflecting institutionalized power. However, for Dickie, the world of art does not identify with a single system of art (that is, with the artistic market). The world of art is for him the totality of all artistic systems and also includes the network of nonconformist artists and thinkers. The levelling on the *status quo*, therefore, is not attributable to the institutional theory of art, but to one of its restrictive and tendentious interpretations. What it requires, instead, is a minimum of sociability. Even genius presupposes the existence, however virtual, of a public or of a very small circle of admirers. And even the art of madmen is inscribed in a network of people and institutions who are concerned about them.

In spite of its rejection of a metaphysical essence of art, conceptual art remains, nonetheless, anchored to the idea of an identity of art. This becomes mobile, variable, in progress, but always determinable. In Kosuth's case it even assumes the character of a tautology: 'The works of art,' he writes, 'are analytical propositions. That is, viewed within their context, as art, they do not provide information of any kind on concrete data' (K 26). Conceptual art, therefore, emerges as an operation without residue, which aims at conquering the truth of tautology which, according to Wittgenstein, has its own unsubstantial certainty. In fact, tautology is unconditionally true and 'does not stand in any representational relation to reality' [4.462].[92] It can be formalized in the expression: 'If p, then p; and if q, then q' from which is evident that there is no residue. In this fashion, Kosuth aspires to a transparent art. I find particularly meaningful the fact that he devotes great attention to water, because it is formless and colourless.

Moving in a completely different way, even institutional theory promotes a tautological idea of art. In this case, tautology does not derive from a will to annul ties between art and reality, but, on the contrary, from a tendency to level art on the existent, conferring upon it an institutional character. It is not a question, therefore, of logical tautology but of social circularity between art, artists and the world of art, each referring to the other. Even in this case there is no residue!

Kosuth's thinking has been investigated and developed by the French philosopher Jean-François Lyotard. In introducing Kosuth's work, Lyotard points out that the inscriptions that appear in Kosuth's works of art are not at all transparent or tautological, as its theory would have us believe. 'Kosuth's work is a meditation on writing,' writes Lyotard,[93] and 'writing conceals some gesture, a remainder of gesture, beyond readability' (K 16). In fact the written phrase is never transparent as a glass or faithful as a mirror. 'Thought is art because it yearns to make "present" the other meanings that it conceals and that it does not think. There is, in art as in thought, an outburst, the desire to present or signify to the limit the totality of meanings' (K 16). Therefore whoever says remainder says excess. 'This excess in art and in thought denies the evidence of the given, excavates the readable' and shows 'that all is not said, written or presented' (K 16).

This passage by Lyotard is particularly important as it singles out a point where art and philosophy come together and are no longer in competition with one another. There is no longer any sense in considering philosophy as the *after* of art (as Hegel and the Situationists thought), or, on the contrary, to consider art as the *after* of philosophy (as Kosuth and conceptual art believe). Philosophy and art meet in the fact of not being reducible to a complete totality, or to a tautology. The accounts never balance out. There is always a difference that shows up now as remainder now as excess. In short, in philosophy and in art we always have to do with a plus or a minus. This is the difference of philosophy and art with respect to the banality of what is equal to itself. Lyotard writes that 'Writing leaves the remainder to be written, by the mere fact that it writes. There will always be a remainder' (K 16).

After all, both Situationists and Kosuth claim to abolish any opacity, the former in the absolute transparency of critical theory, the latter in the absolute evidence of tautology. Lyotard shows that this presumption is naive. 'The perceptible is not entirely perceived; the visual is more than the visible.' 'The visible and readable tautology, *This is a sentence*, insinuates the necessarily unreadable antinomy, *This is not a sentence, but a thing*' (K 16). Therefore, philosophy and art meet in the experience of an excess or a remainder, which is revealed to be as opaque and impenetrable as a *thing*! The *thing* is not only an external entity with respect to philosophy and art, but has insinuated itself in the very substance of philosophical writing and of the conceptual work.

Thus, Lyotard has broken the tautological circularity of conceptual art by showing the inevitable emergence of a remainder. Something similar occurs also for the institutional theory of art which, not unlike Kosuth's, excludes the possibility of a remainder. Here the rupture of the tautological circle was accomplished by the French sociologist Nathalie Heinich, according to whom the play of contemporary art cannot be limited to the mediators, to whom eventually the artists are added.[94] There is a remainder to which the

institutional theory of art does not give the necessary attention:
the public. And today when one says 'public' one does not imply
the narrow elite of traditional experts or the traditional museum-
goer, which Bourdieu has included under the category of social
distinction. The 'happy few', respectful followers of the religion of
art, have been replaced by a mass of blasphemous people who are
indifferent to the provocations of contemporary art, or even, more
often, to open rejection. Between contemporary art and the large
majority of the population, a frightening cultural gap has opened up,
which is manifested in a series of reactions that go from irony to the
accusation of squandering public money. The relation between
contemporary art and the public is no longer structured, therefore,
on the demand for recognition and admiration, but on provocation
and scandal. Artistic value, therefore, is based more on the market of
information and communication than on the cultural one. The
blasphemous public, in whose tow we find traditional critics and
intellectuals, intervenes in the determination of what is art precisely
through its rejection. In fact, as Nathalie Heinich remarks, the
plastic arts have been for centuries under the sign of transgression
and defiance. Their unpopularity plays a very important role in the
determination of their status. In the last few decades, institutions and
administrators, who once shared with the great public the rejection
of artistic provocation, now tend to be on the side of the artists and
favour the outbreak of scandals, because they gain from them a
benefit in publicity measurable in journalistic notoriety and crowds
of visitors to exhibitions. The avant-garde appears to be the winner
not so much on the level of the market of art (as was the case up to
the 1980s), but at the institutional level. It succeeded in finding
an ally in the administration, but leaves something out. This
remainder is precisely the great blasphemous public that becomes,
even if in an ironic and paradoxical way, the key to the success of
artistic operations.

   The relation between aesthetic judgement and democracy is
reversed. What is aesthetically interesting is not what public opinion
likes, but precisely what irritates and scandalizes it. Therefore, even
on the sociological side art is not a tautology. It does not reduce to
what the institutions and the world of art say it is. There is an opaque
sociological remainder that does not belong to the world of art and
that intervenes actively, even if negatively, to the determination of its
status. Thus, following the problematic of conceptual art in its two

aspects, the analytical and the sociological, one arrives at the same conclusions. Art is not identical to itself.

4. *Art as Crypt*

The overall artistic experiences of the 1990s that can be grouped under the label of *Post human* are characterized by the aim of transgressing the frontiers that separate art from reality. With them, the question of the relation between art and philosophy has taken a further step with respect to the way in which the Situationists and Conceptualists posed the problem. In fact, if art tends to erase those symbolical screens that sheltered it from direct comparison with reality, it finds itself on the same ground as philosophy, which has always claimed to be in close relation to reality, even if through the mediation of the concept. But even this difference is reduced when we keep in mind the tendency of more recent philosophy to focus its attention precisely on what is on this side or on that side of the concept, on what is heterogeneous and irreducible to a firm conceptual hold. As a result of relinquishing their traditional ground, both art and philosophy find themselves exposed to the danger of banality, of being homogenized, if not trivialized. In their effort of wanting to maintain a relation with society, they now experience the erosion of the specificity of their message and, what is still more serious, they risk being replaced by more accessible and commercial imitations, according to the old maxim: 'the bad coin chases the good one.' To offset these calamities, they have at least one card left to play, the card of the *remainder*, that is, the idea that there is in art as in philosophy something which is irreducible to the processes of normalization and standardization at work in society.

This strategy, however, entails a reflection on the notion of *remainder* that goes in the opposite direction to the one meant by the Situationists and the Conceptualists. *Remainders,* for them, are the works of art with respect to something more important and essential than the situation or the idea. In this sense, the *remainder* implies a state of inferiority or inadequacy with respect to something to which one attributes greater value. The works of art are conceived as a parasitic surplus with respect to the artistic activity which is manifested par excellence in the event or in invention.

This position, however, turned out to be very dangerous for the future of art and philosophy. In fact, event and invention run the risk of being thought of within a vitalist, or even a functionalist perspective that denies legitimacy to what is not dissolved in biological or efficient procedures. This way of thinking is at work in some theories of communication that compare society to a living organism,[95] and art to a stream whose flow is hindered by works of art. Therefore, the *remainder* is thought of as *fetish*, the object of condemnation both aesthetic and moral.[96] The Greek verb *leípo,* and its derivatives, corresponds to this meaning which underlies lack, absence, abandonment. It corresponds to the Latin *linquo* from which derive many Italian words with very different meanings: *delinquente* (criminal, delinquent), *reliquia* (relic), *deliquio* (swoon, fainting).

But *remainder* can also be understood in the opposite sense, as related to the Latin word *restus* (from *sto*), referring to the idea of stability, steadiness and resistance. Under this aspect, the remainder of art would be what in artistic experience is opposed to, and resists, homogenization, conformity, the processes of mass consensus at work in contemporary society and, more generally, the tendency of reducing the greatness and dignity of art. This trend, however, does not move at all towards the rehabilitation of the work of art understood as *monument*. Implicit in the notion of *remainder* is an anti-monumental and anti-classical position. If art is *remainder*, it means that the idea of the work of art as somewhat harmonic and reconciled must be left behind because art is crossed by internal tensions, conflicts and fractures. If art is *remainder*, it means that the whole does not hold, does not stand, but breaks up in asymmetrical elements, deeply discordant among each other. The polemic against communicative reductionism, therefore, does not imply a return to an art of works of art, or toward a metaphysical conception of art and philosophy.

In fact, we must not forget that the contemporary situation of art and philosophy is the result of the end of classicism and the collapse of metaphysics. It is connected with that event that Nietzsche called the 'death of God', namely, the decline of all aesthetic, moral, and cognitive certainties elaborated by humanity to overcome fear and to confer some kind of certainty to the life of the individual and the community. In fact, this condition was considered by Nietzsche as the premise of *nihilism*.

As is well-known, Freud has provided the most profound analysis of the emotional state caused by the loss of a loved one and of an abstraction that has taken its place.[97] The psychic events generated by this state can be quite different, according to Freud. Only the 'work of mourning' makes possible the psychic elaboration that allows the progressive withdrawal of the libido from the loved one and to shift it onto other objects of the external world. If this shift does not occur, a melancholia can set in, characterized by deep disheartenment and by a loss of the ability to love, and by a dejection of the self which is expressed in self-reproaches and in a deep-rooted feeling of guilt. For Freud, melancholy is the result of the failure of the 'work of mourning'. If it does not take place, a pathological syndrome sets in whereby, together with an enormous impoverishment of the I, there is an attitude of accusation with regard to others.

This analysis of melancholia provides a key to understanding *nihilism*, which is a melancholic reaction to the decline and disappearance of those metaphysical 'values' that have sustained and supported the rise of art and philosophy as cultural guides of the West. With respect to the loss of these 'values', Western culture has not been able to play out the work of mourning, that is, of detaching progressively from its metaphysical foundation by rethinking the 'greatness' of art and philosophy, in a manner adequate to the new historical, social and economic conditions. Without knowing it, Western culture continues to be possessed by the past, and reverts on itself the guilt of its disappearance, because it identifies subconsciously with it. A profoundly pathological picture of culture and art is the result. On the one hand, it is manifested in a feeling of profound self-inadequacy that turns to self-denigration and abjection, on the other hand, in the inability of believing anyone else worthy of esteem and admiration. Art and philosophy remain, thus, prisoners of those metaphysical 'values' that they negate in words. Their *nihilism* (or *cynicism*) is not a liberation from tradition, not a phenomenon of disenchantment and secularization, on the contrary, it is the indolence of decadent and melancholic gentlemen who are no longer capable of finding their place in the general re-negotiation of all the greatness inherent in the process of globalization. Today's *nihilists* (or *cynics*) are not at all the heirs of the *esprit forts* and *dandies* of past centuries. They are melancholic people incapable of recycling themselves, and inserting themselves in the new hierarchy of greatness.

After all, the negation of 'values' worked out by *nihilism* is something closer to that mechanism described by Freud as *negation (Verneinung)*. It consists of expressing negatively a thought whose existence has been removed.[98] In the specific case of *nihilism*, the assertion of traditional 'values' can only enter consciousness on condition that they be negated. These 'values' cannot be expressed positively because they would reveal the negative value of those who advocate them, their 'inability' to cope with what they claim. At the same time, however, these values cannot be completely expelled from their psychic reality, because that would require the elaboration of new criteria of evaluation. In other words, the melancholic nihilist, rather than confronting his own inadequacy, prefers to negate the validity of the new. Thus the world of art and philosophy is crowded with melancholic people who have 'great scorn' for themselves and the world because they can only prolong psychically the existence of what has lost 'value'. Freud remarks that melancholy belongs to the psychic constellation of rebellion, but the revolt of the melancholic will never be a revolution because it is rather a complaint with regard to something which is lacking, a complaint that becomes an accusation towards those who do not share his melancholy.

An original development of Freud's notions of mourning and melancholia is given by Nicholas Abraham and Maria Torok in *The Shell and the Kernel* (1987), a collection of essays written in the previous decade. Referring to the idea of a pupil of Freud, Sándor Ferenczi, they explain the labour of grief with the phenomenon of *introjection*. The trauma of loss can be overcome through an extension of the interests of the Self which enriches itself with new perspectives by transferring the libido onto other objects, while maintaining the memory of the past. Completely different from this process, instead, is the phenomenon of *incorporation*, which they determine quite singularly. While introjection represents a growth of the self, in incorporation an extraneous psychic entity is installed within the Self, in an almost magical and instantaneous way, endowed with its own autonomy that remains unknown to whoever is carrying it within. It constitutes 'a sort of artificial unconscious', different from the dynamic unconscious of psychoanalytical tradition.[99] This entity is similar to a secret tomb, a crypt, which preserves as if it were dead something that it is still living and secretly working.

Cryptic incorporation is a third destiny of mourning which is clearly distinct not only from the labour of grief (introjection), but also from melancholy. In fact, the cryptophore, that is, the person who carries the crypt within himself, also conceals to himself the fact of having lost something. He masks the wound, because it is unsayable: 'since its simple enunciation in words would be lethal for the entire place'. What is being concealed by this complex device? Contrary to what one may think, it is not an absence, a lack, a deficit, but, on the contrary, a pleasure that cannot be recognized as such, which cannot be named because it is an attack not on the dignity of the subject, but on the disappeared character who played the function of an ideal Self. In fact, there has been a loss but it is such that it cannot be recognized and, even less, communicated. The crypt, therefore, takes on the dimension of a remainder, understood not as residue, but as psychic reality, 'reality block', 'topography of reality'.

The phenomenon of cryptic incorporation, described by Abraham and Torok, was analysed by Jacques Derrida in *Fors* (1976),[100] where he discusses the singularity of a space that can be defined as internal and external at the same time. In fact, the crypt is 'a place *enclosed* in another but rigorously separated from it, isolated by the general space through walls, a fence, an *enclave*'.[101] It is an example of 'intestine exclusion' or of 'clandestine inclusion'. For Derrida, it is the forming of a compromise, a conflict which is installed with violence and cannot be resolved. It is the only way of loving without killing and of killing in order not to love. It is the general theatre of a manoeuvre performed to prevent contradictions from turning into catastrophe.

But the most disquieting aspect of cryptic incorporation, which is only hinted at by Abraham and Torok, and by Derrida, is its brightness, its splendour, the glittering of something that cannot be simply explained with the linguistic confusion between *glance* and *glowing* (*glanz*).[102] The crypt, in fact, is a kind of realized utopia, which for this reason must be kept quiet, lest the conflict resumes. It is a hidden treasure that shines only in the dark.

The notion of cryptic incorporation provides the possibility of thinking a third way out of the situation opened up by the 'collapse of values' and 'the death of God'. It shows that it is possible to escape the melancholic cynicism in which art and philosophy seem to have irreparably fallen, even at the price of plunging them into a crypt which is very difficult to enter. At least, this way, they are protected both by the fanatics of 'works of art' and by the fanatics of communication. From this perspective, the task of the philosopher-artist is similar to the cemetery guard, so magnificently described by

Abraham and Torok: 'He stands there, keeping an eye on the comings and goings of the members of its immediate family who – for various reasons – might claim access to the tomb. When he agrees to let in some curious or injured parties, or detectives, he carefully provides them with false leads and fake graves. Those who have visiting privileges will be variously manoeuvred and manipulated. [. . .] Clearly, the career of a cemetery guard – who has to adapt to a varied crowd – is made of guile, ingenuity, and diplomacy.'[103]

Notes

Chapter One

1 Gillo Dorfles, *Fatti e fattoidi. Gli pseudoeventi nell'arte e nella società* (Vicenza: Neri Pozza, 1997).

2 Luigi Pareyson, *Ontologia della libertà* (Torino: Einaudi, 1995), p. 404.

3 Ibid., p. 405.

4 Slavoj Žižek, *The Indivisible Remainder. An Essay on Schelling and Related Matters* (London: Verso, 1996).

5 Dylan Evans, *An Introductory Dictionary of Lacanian Psychoanalysis* (London–New York: Routledge, 1996).

6 Hal Foster, *The Return of the Real* (Cambridge, Mass.: The MIT Press, 1996).

7 Aurel Kolnai, *Der Ekel* (1929) (Tübingen: Max Niemeyer Verlag, 1974).

8 Pareyson, *Ontologia della libertà*, p. 410.

9 Jacques Lacan, *The Ethics of Psychoanalysis (1959–1960) The Seminar of Jacques Lacan, Book VII*, tr. by Dennis Porter (New York–London: W. W. Norton & Co., 1997).

10 Evans, *An Introductory Dictionary of Lacanian Psychoanalysis*, p. 205.

11 Clément Rosset, *Le réel. Traité de l'idiotie* (Paris: Minuit, 1977).

12 Robert Musil, 'On Stupidity' in *Precision and Soul. Essays and Addresses,* ed. and tr. by Burton Pike and David S. Luft (Chicago and London: The University of Chicago Press, 1990), pp. 268–86.

13 Evans, *An Introductory Dictionary of Lacanian Psychoanalysis*, p. 191.

14 Pareyson, *Ontologia della libertà*, p. 425.

15 Evans, *An Introductory Dictionary of Lacanian Psychoanalysis,* p. 133.

16 Ibid., p. 175.

17 Sarah F. Maclaren, 'Magnificenza, lusso, spreco' in *Ágalma* 2 (2002) 43–62.

Chapter Two

18 Jacques Derrida, *The Truth in Painting*, tr. by G. Bennington and I. McLeod. (Chicago and London: The University of Chicago Press, 1987).

19 Gilles Deleuze, *Francis Bacon. Logique de la sensation* (Paris: Editions de la différence, 1984).

20 Roland Barthes, *The Pleasure of the Text*, tr. by Richard Miller (New York: Hill and Wang, 1975). [I have translated *jouissance* with *bliss* in conformity to Miller's translation.]

21 Roland Barthes, *Oeuvres Complètes,* III (Paris: Seuil: 1994–95), p. 158.

22 Mario Perniola is referring to his discussion of masochism in *Il sex appeal dell'inorganico* (Torino: Einaudi, 1994), 52ff. [The English translation of this work is expected from Continuum in 2004.]

23 Barthes, *The Pleasure of the Text*, p. 65.

24 Mario Perniola, *Il sex appeal dell'inorganico* (Torino: Einaudi, 1994).

25 Mario Perniola, *Enigmas. The Egyptian Moment in Society and Art*, tr. by Christopher Woodall (London–New York: Verso, 1995).

26 Roberto Calasso, *L'impuro folle* (Milan: Adelphi, 1974). See also Daniel Paul Schreber (1842–1911), *Memoirs of my nervous illness*, tr., ed., with intro., notes and discussion by Ida Macalpine and Richard A. Hunter (London: W. Dawson, 1955).

27 Wilhelm Dilthey, *Die drei Epochen der modernen Aesthetik und ihre heutige Aufgabe*, in VI *Gesammelte Schriften* (Stuttgart–Göttingen: Teubner & Vandenhoeck & Ruprecht, 1892).

28 György Lukács, *The Meaning of Contemporary Realism*, tr. by John and Necke Mander (London: Merlin Press, 1962).

29 Bret Easton Ellis, *American Psycho* (New York: Vintage Press, 1991).

30 James Ellroy, *My Dark Places* (New York: Random House, 1996).

31 Jeffrey Deitch, ed., *Post human* (Rivoli: Castello di Rivoli, 1992); *Hors limites. L'art et la vie* (Paris: Centre Georges Pompidou, 1994); *Sensation* (London: Royal Academy of Arts, 1997).

32 Teresa Macrí, *Il corpo postorganico* (Milan: Costa & Nolan, 1996).

33 Julia Kristeva, *Powers of Horror: An Essay on Abjection*, tr. by Leon S. Roudiez. (New York: Columbia University Press, 1982).

34 Roland Barthes, *Oeuvres Complètes*. III, 887.

35 Ibid., 794.

36 Ibid., 893.

37 Ibid., 143.

Chapter Three

38 David Harvey, *The Condition of Postmodernity. An Enquiry into the Origins of Cultural Change* (Oxford: Blackwell, 1990).

39 Jean-François Lyotard, *The Postmodern Condition: A Report on Knowledge*, tr. by Geoff Bennington and Brian Massumi (Minneapolis: The University of Minnesota Press, 1979).

40 Jean-François Lyotard, *The Postmodern Explained. Correspondence 1982–1985*, tr. and ed. by Julian Pefanis and Morgan Thomas. Afterword by Wlad Godzich (Minneapolis–London: University of Minnesota Press, 1993), p. 80.

41 Andy Warhol, *The Philosophy of Andy Warhol (From A to B and Back Again)* (New York: Harcourt Brace, 1975).

42 Linda Hutcheon, *Irony's Edge, The Theory and Politics of Irony*. (London–New York: Routledge, 1994).

43 Jean-François Lyotard, *The Differend. Phrases in Dispute*, tr. by Georges Van Den Abbeele (Minneapolis: University of Minnesota Press, 1988).

44 Jean Baudrillard, *Le Complot de l'art* (Paris: Sens & Tonka, 1997).

45 Jean-François Lyotard, *The Postmodern Explained* (Minnesota: University of Minnesota Press, 1992).

Chapter Four

46 Roberto Nepoti, *Storia del documentario* (Bologna: Patron, 1988).
47 Ivelise Perniola, 'Le parole hanno un senso …' in *Bianco e Nero*, LXI, 1–2 (January–April 2000).
48 Gilles Deleuze, *The Fold. Leibniz and the Baroque,* tr. by Tom Conley (Minneapolis and London: University of Minnesota Press, 1993).
49 The screenplay of the film is included in Guy Debord, *Oeuvres cinematographiques complètes* (Paris: Champs Libre, 1978).
50 Kristine Stiles, 'Shaved Heads and Marked Bodies. Representations from Cultures of Trauma' in *Lusitania* 6 (1994).
51 Tiziana Villani, 'Linciaggi' in *La Balena Bianca* 6 (1993).
52 Paolo Chiozzi, *Manuale di antropologia visiva* (Milan: Unicopli, 1993).
53 Erich Neumann, *The Great Mother: An Analysis of the Archetype,* tr. by Ralph Manheim (Princeton, N.J.: Princeton University Press, 1972).
54 Henry Havelock Ellis, 'Undinism' in *Studies in the Psychology of Sex*. Vol III. (New York: Random House, 1936), pp. 376–476.
55 Denis Diderot, *Letter on the Deaf and Dumb* in *Diderot's Early Philosophical Works,* tr. and ed. by Margaret Jourdain (Chicago and London: The Open Court Publishing Co., 1916).
56 Siegfried Kracauer, *Theory of Film. The redemption of Physical Reality* (London– New York: Oxford University Press, 1960).
57 Ludwig Wittgenstein, *Remarks on the Philosophy of Psychology,* 2 vols., tr. by G. E. M. Anscombe. (Oxford: Basil Blackwell, 1980).

Chapter Five

58 Walter Benjamin, 'The Work of Art in the Age of Mechanical Reproduction' in *Illuminations* (New York: Schocken Books, 1969).
59 Benjamin, 'Epilogue' to 'The Work of Art'.
60 Pierre Bourdieu, 'Une interprétation de la théorie de la religion selon Max Weber' in *Archives Européennes de Sociologie* XII (1971) 1.
61 Georges Didi-Huberman, *Ce que nous voyons, ce qui nous regarde* (Paris: Minuit, 1992).
62 Nathalie Heinich, *Le triple jeu de l'art contemporain.* (Paris: Minuit, 1998).
63 Friedrich Nietzsche, *The Wanderer and His Shadow. Human all too Human,* tr. by R. J. Hollingdale (Cambridge: Cambridge University Press, 1996).
64 Gianni Vattimo, *Il soggetto e la maschera. Nietzsche e il problema della liberazione* (Milan: Bompiani, 1974).
65 Ibid., p. 141.
66 Nathalie Heinich, *Ce que l'art fait à la sociologie* (Paris: Minuit, 1998).
67 John Frow, *Cultural Studies and Cultural Value* (Oxford: Clarendon Press, 1995) pp. 10–11.
68 Frow, 131ff.
69 Vattimo, *Il soggetto e la maschera,* p. 140.
70 Luc Boltanski and Laurent Thévenot, *De la justification. Les économies de la grandeur* (Paris: Gallimard, 1991).

71 Ibid., p. 414.
72 Ibid., p. 413.
73 Ibid., p. 290.
74 Ibid., p. 201–2.
75 Heinich, *Ce que l'art fait à la sociologie,* p. 21.
76 Ibid., p. 24.
77 Boltanski and Thévenot, *De la justification. Les economies de la grandeur,* p. 266.

Chapter Six

78 Mario Perniola, *Disgusti. Le nuove tendenze estetiche* (Milan: Costa & Nola, 1998).
79 Guy Debord, *Oeuvres cinématographiques complètes.*
80 Guy Debord, *Comments on the Society of the Spectacle,* tr. by Malcolm Imrie (London–New York: Verso, 1998). Also, Guy Debord, *The Society of the Spectacle,* tr. by Donald Nicholson-Smith (New York: Zone Books, 1995).
81 Debord, *Comments on the Society of the Spectacle.*
82 Carlo Diano, *Forma ed evento. Principii per una interpretazione del mondo greco* (Venice: Marsilio, 1994).
83 Carlo Diano, *Linee per una fenomenologia dell'arte* (Venice: Neri Pozza, 1956), p. 12.
84 Aldo Magris, *L'idea di destino nel pensiero antico.* 2 vols. (Udine: Del Bianco, 1984), p. 139.
85 Mario Perniola, *I situazionisti* (Rome: Castelvecchi, 1998), pp. 155–71.
86 Magris, *L'idea di destino nel pensiero antico,* p. 294.
87 Magris, p. 297, note 124.
88 Gianni Carchia, *L'estetica antica* (Roma–Bari: Laterza, 1999), p. 137.
89 Mario Perniola, *Transiti* (Roma: Castelvecchi, 1998). This work is partially translated in Mario Perniola, *Ritual Thinking: Sexuality, Death, World,* tr. by Massimo Verdicchio. Foreword by Hugh J. Silverman (Amherst: Humanity Press, 2001).
90 Joseph Kosuth, *Art after Philosophy and After. Collected Writings 1966–1990,* ed., with Intro. by Gabriele Guercio. Foreword by Jean-François Lyotard (Cambridge, Mass.: The MIT Press, 1991), p. 18. Further references to this work will be in the text as K plus page number.
91 George Dickie, *The Art Circle: A Theory of Art* (New York: Havens, 1984).
92 Ludwig Wittgenstein, *Tractatus logico-philosophicus* (1921), tr. by D. F. Pears and B. F. McGuinness (London: Routledge & Kegan Paul; New York: the Humanities Press, 1961).
93 See Jean-François Lyotard, 'Foreword: After The Words', foreword to Joseph Kosuth, *Art after Philosophy and After. Collected Writings 1966–1990.*
94 Heinich, *Le triple jeu de l'art contemporain.*
95 Arman Mattelart, *L'invention de la communication* (Paris: La Découverte, 1994).
96 Sergio Benvenuto, 'L'orrore discreto del feticismo' in *Àgalma* 1(2000), 29–39.
97 Sigmund Freud, 'Mourning and Melancholia' (1917) in *Collected Papers* IV, ed. by Joan Riviere (New York: Basic Books, Inc., 1959), 152ff.
98 Sigmund Freud, 'Negation' (1925), in *Collected Papers* V, ed. by James Strachey (New York: Basic Books, Inc., 1959) 181ff.

99 Nicholas Abraham and Maria Torok, *The Wolf Man's Magic Word. A Cryptonymy,* tr. by Nicholas Rand. Foreword by Jacques Derrida (Minnesota: The University of Minnesota Press, 1994).

100 The essay by Jacques Derrida, 'Fors: The English Words of Nicolas Abraham and Maria Torok', tr. by Barbara Johnson, appears as Foreword to Abraham and Torok's *The Wolf Man's Magic Word.* Derrida's essay is also published as 'Fors' in *The Georgia Review* 31 (1977), 64–116.

101 Nicholas Abraham and Maria Torok, *The Shell and the Kernel* (Chicago: The University of Chicago Press, 1994).

102 Sigmund Freud, 'Fetishism' (1927) in *Collected Papers* IV, ed. by James Strachey (New York: Basic Books, Inc., 1959) 198ff.

103 Nicholas Abraham and Maria Torok, 'The Topography of Reality: Sketching a Metapsychology of Secrets' in *The Shell and the Kernel. Renewals of Psychoanalysis,* Vol. I, ed., tr., and with introduction by Nicholas T. Rand (Chicago & London: The University of Chicago Press, 1994), 159. [I have altered the passage slightly to conform to Perniola's text which replaces the 'ego' with 'the philosopher-artist'.]

Mario Perniola's Books in English

– *Enigmas. The Egyptian Moment in Society and Art,* tr. by Christopher Woodall (London and New York: Verso, 1995).
– *Ritual Thinking. Sexuality, Death, World,* tr. by Massimo Verdicchio. Foreword by Hugh J. Silverman (Amherst: Humanity Books, 2001).
– *Art and Its Shadow*, tr. by Massimo Verdicchio. Foreword by Hugh J. Silverman (London and New York: Continuum, 2003).
– *The Sex Appeal of the Inorganic*, tr. by Massimo Verdicchio. Foreword by Hugh J. Silverman (London and New York: Continum, 2004).

Index of Names

39331111R00057

Made in the USA
Lexington, KY
17 February 2015